UNIVERSAL
BASIC INCOME

A complete list of books in this series can be found online at
https://mitpress.mit.edu/books/series/mit-press-essential-knowledge-series.

UNIVERSAL
BASIC INCOME

KARL WIDERQUIST

The MIT Press | Cambridge, Massachusetts | London, England

The MIT Press would like to thank the anonymous peer reviewers who provided comments on drafts of this book. The generous work of academic experts is essential for establishing the authority and quality of our publications. We acknowledge with gratitude the contributions of these otherwise uncredited readers.

This book was set in Chaparral Pro by New Best-set Typesetters Ltd. Printed and bound in the United States of America.

Library of Congress Cataloging-in-Publication Data

Names: Widerquist, Karl, author.
Title: Universal basic income / Karl Widerquist.
Description: Cambridge, Massachusetts : The MIT Press, [2024] | Series: The MIT press essential knowledge series | Includes bibliographical references and index.
Identifiers: LCCN 2023018043 (print) | LCCN 2023018044 (ebook) | ISBN 9780262546898 (paperback) | ISBN 9780262376808 (epub) | ISBN 9780262376792 (pdf)
Subjects: LCSH: Basic income. | Income.
Classification: LCC HC79.I5 W53 2024 (print) | LCC HC79.I5 (ebook) | DDC 339.2—dc23/eng/20230912
LC record available at https://lccn.loc.gov/2023018043
LC ebook record available at https://lccn.loc.gov/2023018044

10 9 8 7 6 5 4 3 2 1

publication supported by a grant from
The Community Foundation for Greater New Haven
as part of the **Urban Haven Project**

CONTENTS

SERIES FOREWORD

The MIT Press Essential Knowledge series offers accessible, concise, beautifully produced pocket-size books on topics of current interest. Written by leading thinkers, the books in this series deliver expert overviews of subjects that range from the cultural and the historical to the scientific and the technical.

In today's era of instant information gratification, we have ready access to opinions, rationalizations, and superficial descriptions. Much harder to come by is the foundational knowledge that informs a principled understanding of the world. Essential Knowledge books fill that need. Synthesizing specialized subject matter for nonspecialists and engaging critical topics through fundamentals, each of these compact volumes offers readers a point of access to complex ideas.

INTRODUCING UNIVERSAL BASIC INCOME

The vast majority of people aren't allowed to use any resources except air and public spaces without the permission of an owner. We can't build a shelter, hunt, gather, fish, farm, start a cooperative, or start our own business without serving (i.e., providing some service for) the people who own the resources we need to do these things. Except for the wealthy few, we are effectively required by law to get a job to earn the money to buy the right to use the resources that were here before any of us and that we're all evolved to depend on.

There is no formal penalty for violating this legal requirement, but the informal penalties include poverty, economic destitution, homelessness, malnutrition, and hunger. If you want to live, you can't just work for yourself, for the needy, or for other nonwealthy people: you have to spend a substantial amount of time serving at least one member of the group of people who own the resources you need to keep you alive.

Throughout this book, I'll use the term *external assets* to mean natural resources and the things we make out of them other than our own human bodies. It's a little broader than the term *physical capital* (which includes only external assets used in the production process) and a little narrower than the term *property* (which might include your body and abilities). I presume we all agree that people have special rights over their own bodies, but I think people have substantial disagreements about whether, how, and under what circumstances natural resources and the external assets we make out of them should become property.

The division of the earth's resources into property has many benefits, but we've done it in a way that gives some people huge shares and others little or nothing. Under the rules we have, the property system has many cruel aspects, including fear, stress, alienation, poverty, burnout, homelessness, and hopelessness. Because most of us have no alternative to some form of paid labor, we are generally willing to accept lower wages, longer work hours, and less appealing work conditions than we otherwise would, and we all go through life with more fear and anxiety than we would need to if we had direct access either to the natural resources we need to survive or to cash compensation large enough to buy access to the external assets we need.

In some situations, people are forced to accept dangerous jobs, sexual harassment, and other forms of abuse from employers or spouses because they need someone with money to keep them alive. That *need* is artificial. It is created by the way our governments choose to allocate access rights to the earth's resources. Many different rules are possible.

Let's consider a way to divide resources that isn't so cruel.

In 1918, Bertrand Russell argued that "a certain small income, sufficient for necessaries, should be secured to all, whether they work or not, and that a larger income . . . should be given to those who are willing to engage in some work which the community recognizes as useful. On this basis we may build further."[1]

Russell's proposal is very much what we know today as *Universal Basic Income* (UBI)—that is, "a periodic cash payment unconditionally delivered to all on an individual basis, without means-test or work requirement."[2] Russell adds that the income is large enough to live on and that the UBI plan will be structured so that people who do things like paid labor end up with more than people who live solely off UBI. Both of these stipulations are important but not always included in the definition of UBI. Ahead, I define UBI in more detail and slightly differently, but Russell's description gives you a very good idea of what it is.

Under a UBI system, we may divide the resources of the earth unequally, but the people who get large shares of resources and the external assets we make out of those resources compensate the people who have gotten little or no share. Compensation has to be unconditional; otherwise, it's not compensation at all—it's a wage.

As Russell mentions, UBI is not all there is to social justice, but it removes one cruel feature built into our economic system. A UBI economy does not use fear as a motivator. A UBI of sufficient size removes the fear of poverty, homelessness, and economic destitution that is built into our system and into most familiar alternative systems. With a UBI of sufficient size, you will always know that no matter what, you will have enough income to cover your basic needs, including housing, food, clothing, and so on.

In many ways, UBI is a mild reform. On its own (without other major changes to the existing system), UBI simply creates a market economy where income doesn't start at zero. It establishes a gapless safety net while leaving the many opportunities of the market in place.

But this mild reform has far-reaching effects.

A UBI large enough to live on necessarily creates a voluntary-participation economy. If we stop using fear as a work incentive, we give everyone the power to say no to paid labor, self-employment, or any other active form of economic participation if they so choose. This aspect makes any economy with a UBI very different from the

UBI simply creates
a market economy
where income doesn't
start at zero.

existing economic system and from most well-known alternatives. Unfettered capitalism puts most people in the position in which they have no other choice but to sell their labor to the people who own physical capital. Karl Marx's vague solution (from each according to their ability, to each according to their needs) seems to imply a fixed work requirement. The nominally Marxist state of the Soviet Union interpreted it that way when its leaders wrote a work requirement into its first constitution. Welfare capitalism and social democracy sometimes have generous benefits, but those benefits are usually conditional on economic participation or on proof that beneficiaries are unable to participate.

That is, all of these very diverse economic systems include mandatory-participation requirements. I start with this issue because it calls attention to the question behind the question of whether to introduce UBI. Should we have a mandatory-participation economy or a voluntary-participation economy? Should everyone get an income—even people who could take jobs but choose not to?

I think that question immediately divides most readers into two groups even if their answers are only tentative: Yes, because no one deserves to live in poverty or homelessness. No, because everyone who can work must work, or—more realistically—everyone who isn't wealthy and can work must work. The (sometimes almost instinctive) commitment to mandatory participation is, I believe, the central source of opposition to UBI, and so the choice between mandatory and voluntary participation comes up repeatedly throughout this book in one form or another.

A voluntary-participation economy is possible. Later chapters show that UBI isn't terribly expensive, and it leaves plenty of room for incentives. The market system won't fall apart the moment we stop using the threat of economic destitution to keep low-income people working. If jobs need doing, we have enormous ability to get people to work by offering good salaries, good working conditions, advancement opportunities, respect, and access to the many luxuries our economy is capable of producing. If you need the background threat of homelessness and hunger to get people to do the job you want them to do for the wages you're willing to pay, maybe your job doesn't need to be done at all.

A livable UBI eliminates poverty. Poverty is not the failure to meet one's basic needs, it is the inability to *afford* to meet one's basic needs, and this book will argue that only UBI—or something very similar—can eliminate poverty.

We define *homelessness* as the mere fact of not being housed, rather than the inability to afford housing, but very few of the half-million homeless people in the United States are on the street for any other reason, and so I tend to use homelessness synonymously with the inability to afford housing. In that sense, UBI can eliminate homelessness. The few remaining rough sleepers will probably fall into two categories: either they are making a rational

A livable UBI eliminates poverty.

choice and should probably be left alone, or they have a mental disability and should probably be helped in a way appropriate for their condition.

We can point to many proximate causes of poverty and homelessness: this person made foolish decisions; that person ran away from an abusive home. But there is only one ultimate cause of the inability to afford the resources one needs for a decent life: rules that limit access to resources. We can change those rules, if we're ready to introduce a voluntary-participation economy.

A voluntary-participation economy is a humane economy. It ends the cruel treatment of people at the bottom and relieves the fear of people in the middle. It invites everyone to participate in our productive system by offering access to the luxuries it can create.

UBI has inspired a growing worldwide movement, which is stronger as I write these words than it has been since Thomas Spence wrote the oldest-known argument for it in 1797. Although UBI isn't the only reform that the existing economic system needs, millions of people are coming to believe that it is one of the most important and fundamental reforms we need right now.

The UBI movement grows out of frustration with increasingly precarious employment; with growing inequality and uncertainty; with increasingly unaffordable housing; with stagnant wages and salaries; and with persistent hunger, homelessness, and poverty. Perhaps most important of all, the UBI movement grows out of frustration with the ineffectiveness and political vulnerability of conventional policies that attempt to address our economic and social problems without eliminating mandatory participation.

The primary goal of this book is to explain the essentials of UBI: what it is, how it works, the state of research into it, the most popular arguments for and against it, how much it costs, how it can be financed, its likely effects, its history, and its possible future.

But, as I'm sure you've already guessed, I am a strong supporter of UBI. And so, this book's secondary goal is to convince readers that UBI is a good, workable idea that should be enacted all around the world. I will make this argument in a way that explains and addresses both sides of the debate over whether to introduce it. Whether you agree with my position on UBI or not, I think you can learn more from a passionate and honest attempt to argue the strongest points for it and refute the strongest points against it than from a dispassionate list of points on either side.

With this in mind, I proceed to a more thorough definition of UBI.

UBI Defined by Five Essential Characteristics

UBI—also called Unconditional Basic Income, Basic Income, citizen's income, citizen's basic income, the social dividend, demogrant, and many other names—is defined by the Basic Income Earth Network (BIEN; formerly the Basic Income European Network) as "a periodic cash payment unconditionally delivered to all on an individual basis, without means-test or work requirement." I was a cochair of BIEN when that definition was adopted. I thought the negotiations that produced it were a great example of positive compromise. BIEN's definition includes the following five essential characteristics:

1. *Periodic:* UBI is paid at regular intervals (e.g., daily, weekly, or monthly). A one-time grant is not a UBI.

2. *In cash:* UBI is paid in the appropriate medium of exchange for the community so that people can decide what to spend it on. It is not, therefore, paid in-kind (such as in vouchers for food or other goods and services).

3. *Individual:* UBI is paid separately to each person rather than jointly to a household. It remains the same whether individuals form households or live separately. Although the UBIs of young children or people with severe mental disabilities would be entrusted to their parent or guardian, neither spouse is given control of the entire family's UBI.

4. *Universal:* UBI is paid to every member of a political community (such as a nation or a region) or every resident of a geographic area without any means-test.

People get the same UBI regardless of income, wealth, earnings capacity, family composition, and so on. Although financially better-off people might pay more in taxes than they receive in UBI, they receive the same UBI as everyone else.

5. *Unconditional:* UBI is paid without a requirement to work, to demonstrate willingness to work, to demonstrate the inability to work, or to meet any requirements other than membership in a political or geographic community.

Strictly speaking, the conditions of *universality* and *unconditionality* are synonymous. If a program has any conditions, some people will not receive it, and therefore it will not be universal. If a program is nonuniversal for any reason, there are some conditions under which people fail to receive it. For that reason, *Universal Basic Income* and *Unconditional Basic Income* are used interchangeably as names for this idea, but the emphasis of the two terms provides clarification. *Unconditionality* emphasizes UBI's lack of work- or desert-based requirements. *Universality* emphasizes its lack of means testing. A *means test* is any restriction on a payment based on an assessment of whether the recipient needs it or not. Traditional redistributive programs often deny payments because people have high income or wealth or earnings capacity.

Later chapters discuss why UBI has these characteristics.

Three More Desirable Characteristics of UBI

Most UBI supporters believe that a desirable UBI would also have at least three additional characteristics: it would be lifelong, structured so that people are financially better off earning more private income, and enough to cover basic needs. These were left out of BIEN's official definition of UBI, perhaps because they went without saying or because they were considered nonessential. The following three subsections discuss these characteristics. A fourth subsection discusses several other characteristics that supporters occasionally suggest.

Lifelong

Strictly speaking, to be both regular and universal, a payment must be lifelong, and most UBI supporters believe it should be. Whether a temporary universal payment (say, weekly for one year during a recession) qualifies as UBI is controversial. There may be practical reasons to have lower payments for children and higher payments for elderly people (see "Enough to Cover Basic Needs"), and few UBI supporters would like to say that such a program is *not* a UBI. Even programs solely for working-age adults are sometimes called UBI. Few UBI supporters believe that such a UBI would be ideal, but most would recognize it as a form of UBI.

Structured So That People Are Financially Better-off Earning More Private Income

People who have private income (whether from labor or capital) receive both a UBI and their private income. Although people might pay taxes on their private income, those taxes should be structured so that people who earn more privately always end up with more money overall. If you earn $1.00 while receiving UBI, you might pay a tax on some portion of that $1.00, but you do not have to pay back the full dollar—neither by paying it in taxes nor by losing part of your UBI. As later chapters discuss, many conventional social policies lack this characteristic and give people a perverse incentive to *avoid* making money privately.

This feature is usually left out of the definition, probably for two reasons. First, it is taken for granted because the only way for it *not* to be a characteristic of UBI would be to have a 100 percent tax on private income until taxes matched the size of the UBI, and it would be a very bad idea to have a 100 percent tax on the lowest-income workers. Second, it is not necessary to include this characteristic in the definition to understand what UBI is. There are well-structured UBI programs and badly structured UBI programs. A definition that tried to make it impossible for any badly structured program to fall under the definition of UBI would make for a needlessly wordy and complex definition.

Enough to Cover Basic Needs

Almost everyone in the UBI movement supports a UBI at least high enough to live on. However, UBI supporters disagree about how much is enough and whether that characteristic should be part of the *definition* of UBI. A UBI high enough to live on is sometimes called a *livable* or a *full* UBI, and one smaller than that is sometimes called a *partial* UBI. The lack of a requirement to cover basic needs makes BIEN's definition broader than Bertrand Russell's definition from the first section of this chapter.

I have argued for a livable UBI since I began writing on the issue in the late twentieth century, but I hope I have always made it clear that I see no need to incorporate livability into the definition of UBI. I'm content to define UBI as any nonzero universal grant and to explain that a good UBI must be large enough to live on.

One advantage of leaving livability out is that it makes our definition of UBI consistent with our definitions of most other forms of income. We define a pension as a retirement income and explain that a good one is large enough to live on. We define a salary or a wage as income from labor and explain that a good one is at least enough to live on. We define child support payments as any payment toward the support of a child and explain that a good one provides income large enough to pay the child's living expenses.

People who insist on incorporating the size of the grant into the definition of UBI are, I believe, trying to resolve a political disagreement by definitional fiat. We won't increase support for a livable UBI by telling people who propose a smaller grant that they shouldn't call it UBI in the same way that we won't eliminate bad wages by telling people not to call them wages.

Incorporating livability into the definition of UBI creates at least four problems. First, people disagree about how large an amount is livable. Incorporating livability into the definition invites people who are otherwise allies to accuse each other of not supporting a true UBI. Second, we would not know whether a particular grant was a UBI until we knew the cost of living in an area. Third, a grant's status as a UBI would fluctuate with the cost of living. It might regularly go back and forth between UBI and not UBI if prices are volatile and inflation adjustments come after a lag. Fourth, we would no longer be able to count many UBI experiments, pilot projects, and policies as UBI, and then we would have to explain why these non-UBI policies tell us something about UBI.

One might reasonably ask, if basic needs aren't part of the definition, then what work is the word *basic* doing? Why not call it *universal income*? I believe the word *basic* is a reference to the word *base* rather than to the concept of basic needs. *Universal income* might imply a strict egalitarian policy, such as to each according to their needs. Adding the word *basic* clarifies that people who receive more income in the market end up with a higher overall income than people who make less in the market.

Other Desirable Characteristics

In almost all UBI proposals, the UBI is not considered taxable income, meaning that although many people would pay more in taxes than they receive in UBI, the grant itself is not taxed. Similarly, the UBI cannot be used as collateral for a loan and would be a protected asset in the event of bankruptcy. One is free to give their UBI away the moment they receive it, but the government will enforce no contract binding a person to do so. If one person could pressure another into signing away their UBI, the program would lose many of its desirable effects for promoting equality and combating poverty.

These features give UBI a more truly universal character. However, they usually go without saying because they would otherwise make the definition overly long and technical.

How UBI Differs from Existing Social Policies

UBI would be a major departure from the form of social welfare that has gradually become standard around the world over the last century and a half. Although social welfare systems around the world vary enormously in generosity, most of their programs tend to have one or more of the following characteristics that distinguish them from UBI: categorical, conditional, supervisory, means-tested, and/or in-kind (i.e., delivering benefits in nonmonetary forms). Each of these characteristics conflicts with UBI as defined previously, but they are not necessarily direct opposites of any particular characteristic of UBI. This section explains each of these characteristics, discusses how they conflict with one or more of the five characteristics of UBI's definition, and, by doing so, shows how UBI differs from the conventional approach.

Categorical

Traditional social welfare systems tend to sort low-income people into categories and target different policy combinations for each type of need. The United States has different programs for people who are elderly, temporarily disabled, permanently disabled, unable to find work, taking care of children, working for low wages, and so on.

Some targeting is essential: blind people have different needs than deaf people, for example. But a large portion of our needs (food, shelter, clothing, communication, transportation, etc.) are both common to everyone and readily available in the market to anyone who has money, and so, even if some targeting is necessary, there is room for a substantial in-cash UBI. There is, perhaps, a need for universalism as well, because under the current categorical system, many people with little or no income are not eligible for any of these programs.

If we think about the many different proximate causes of poverty as *the* causes of poverty, it seems to make sense to have a different program for each one. But this strategy ignores the ultimate cause. Because poverty is the inability to afford the resources one needs to live decently, the ultimate cause is the rules that allocate access to resources and the external assets we make out of them. Although we cannot make a rule giving everyone unlimited access to all resources, we can make a rule giving everyone access to enough resources to meet their basic needs by introducing a livable UBI.

With this understood, it becomes clear why programs focusing on the many different proximate causes of poverty often involve victim-blaming and, as I argue ahead, invariably fail to solve the problem.

The central rationale of the categorical approach seems to be less about making sure people with special needs have programs targeted to them and more about separating the "truly needy" or "deserving" poor (whose reasons for being poor are judged acceptable) from the "undeserving" poor (whose reasons are judged unacceptable). The hope is to reduce or eliminate poverty among the "deserving" without reducing the "work incentive" of the people who could work but reject the jobs on offer.

Categorical programs badly fail to achieve these goals. People don't fit neatly into categories. Many people have limited or intermittent ability to work. Many people fluctuate between categories so quickly that the officials who make decisions about them can't keep up. As a consequence, categorical programs tend to leave out many people who fit almost anyone's definition of "truly needy" and end up creating the very work disincentives they were designed to avoid. That is, they create a *poverty trap*: once people qualify, they have a strong incentive to maintain eligibility by refusing what might otherwise be an attractive job.

Economists tend to explain the poverty trap in terms of wages versus lost benefits. But the poverty trap also needs to be understood in terms of risk: both the risk that individuals will be unable to get back on conditional programs if their need returns and the risk that they might need to quit if the boss sexually harasses or otherwise mistreats them. If they quit because of mistreatment, they will be labeled "undeserving" because they "don't want to work."

For these and other reasons, although the effectiveness of welfare systems varies considerably around the world, none fully realizes its ostensible goals. No matter how carefully criteria are drawn, judging people is imperfect. "Deserving" people are left out, and "undeserving" people are included.

Although by almost any moral standard it's better to feed someone who is "underserving" than it is to let a "deserving" person go hungry, government emphasis seems always to be on shutting out potential cheats. Many employed people and many people who meet other categories of "deservingness" remain in poverty. For example, a single parent who works full-time at the federal minimum wage makes $15,080—more than $3,000 below the poverty line for a family of two, $8,000 below the poverty line for a family of three—and will have no money to pay for childcare while at work.

Categorical programs also have costly side effects. A substantial portion of the budget that could go to beneficiaries or to other programs goes instead to the cost of determining eligibility. People who are eligible for programs often wait months or years trying to prove eligibility. Many beneficiaries report being treated like criminals merely for applying for the programs they are eligible for.

Another worrying side effect of the categorical approach is that it punishes children for the behavior of parents. Although some policies are aimed at children, it is impossible to design a system in which "undeserving" parents receive little or no benefits while their deserving children receive enough to keep them out of poverty. And so, millions of children grow up in poverty. They and society bear the costs of it throughout their lives.

UBI avoids many of these issues by meeting everyone's shared basic needs first before categorizing and giving more to people with special needs. One advantage of UBI is that simple policies are more effective in a complex world. Policies that try to match the complexity of the world inevitably become cumbersome, costly, and difficult to comprehend. UBI saves an enormous amount of money lost to the cost of judgement.

UBI has no poverty trap because it doesn't ask people to give up eligibility to earn income privately, and because it ensures after-tax-and-transfer income always increases with private income. But to embrace UBI, we have to give up the desire to force "undeserving" people to work. The most desirable "work incentive" approach is in the eye of the beholder, but UBI is clearly a more effective and humane way to eliminate poverty and promote equality.

Conditional

Fitting into a recognized category of need is not always enough for beneficiaries of traditional social policies. Eligibility rules often require them to do things while receiving benefits or to have done something prior to receiving benefits.

Old-age pensions, unemployment insurance, and disability often require people to have paid into the system for years, but they tend to be relatively free from conditions once beneficiaries begin to receive assistance.

Unemployment benefits in the United States require recipients both to have paid into the system before becoming unemployed and to affirm that they are looking for work while unemployed. Minimum wage laws and some forms of subsidized health insurance require people to accept and keep employment. Other programs require recipients to meet substantial conditions, such as attending counseling or supervisory sessions with a social worker or taking job training courses. Some countries require unemployed people to spend time at job placement centers. Some countries require beneficiaries to refrain from other activities as basic and useful as home maintenance, because it might take time away from their job search.

Conditionality is expensive not only for administrators but also for beneficiaries, who not only have to meet conditions, but also have to do additional work to demonstrate that they have in fact met the conditions. This extra work might sound simple, but it seldom is.

Conditional programs are incapable of eliminating poverty. If the conditions are so lax that no one will fail to meet them, then they aren't real conditions. If the conditions are real, then someone—perhaps many people—will fail to meet them. The US system allows millions of people who fail to meet conditions to experience poverty, horrible working conditions, food insecurity, malnutrition, hunger, housing insecurity, homelessness, vulnerability to abuse, and many other cruelties while their children suffer along with them.

Supervisory

The universal, unconditional nature of UBI necessarily implies that it is also nonsupervisory. That is, no one has to report to a caseworker or follow the instructions of any authority to maintain eligibility for UBI.

Conditional, categorical programs seem to be motivated in part by the belief that low-income people *need* supervision. Many people believe that one of the central causes of poverty is the negative characteristics or bad behavior of the intended beneficiaries: supposedly, they have poor skills, poor work habits, a desire to game the system, and so on.

Based on this belief, the conditions involved in categorical programs usually involve substantial supervision of beneficiaries, to the point that even people who meet the most obvious categories of genuine need find themselves treated like criminals or cheats. Many programs require beneficiaries to meet with a caseworker who has the power to restrict or suspend their benefits. Although the Supplemental Nutrition Assistance Program (SNAP—commonly referred to as *food stamps*) doesn't require beneficiaries to meet with a supervisor, beneficiaries receive a use-restricted debit card that plays a supervisory role by limiting what they can buy even though they might need other things more.

Like categorization and conditionality, supervision is expensive. The government has to pay and train administrators; provide space, forms, computers, and software; and so on. Compliance takes the time of beneficiaries. The constant supervision is demeaning to beneficiaries who have already qualified for the programs. If people are mistaken in the beliefs that poverty stems primarily from the bad behavior of low-income people or that negative sanctions (involving throwing families deeper into poverty) are the most effective way to improve people's behavior, then supervisory programs can be counterproductive.

UBI saves a great deal of resources simply by treating low-income people with respect and relying on positive rewards rather than negative sanctions.

In-Kind

Although many antipoverty programs provide cash benefits, some very important ones (such as SNAP, public housing, and government-subsidized private housing) provide particular goods instead. These programs tend to limit the choices available to recipients. Government-subsidized or government-provided housing, for example, might not be available in the neighborhood the beneficiary would choose if they had an equivalent amount of cash.

UBI gives beneficiaries the freedom to decide which of their needs are most pressing at any given time. UBI reduces the overhead cost associated with in-kind programs. By doing these two things, it delivers more benefit to the recipients for each dollar the government spends.

Not all in-kind benefits can be replaced by a UBI. Housing is so expensive in some parts of the United States that without major real estate market reform, it seems unlikely a UBI could be high enough to replace all forms of housing assistance.

Many other in-kind benefits are not usually associated with income maintenance and cannot be replaced by a UBI. These include public education, public healthcare, public transportation, public libraries, post offices, streets, roads, sidewalks, stoplights, street signs, and so forth. Although these programs can promote economic equality and help to reduce poverty, they are mainly thought of as responses to market failure in those particular markets rather than as responses to poverty and inequality. Few UBI supporters would like to replace many of these programs with a UBI, and so these in-kind programs play little part in our discussion.

Family-Based

Redistributive programs are *individually based* if the benefits are calculated solely on the characteristics of the individual beneficiary in question and benefits are delivered to individuals rather than to one person who represents the family. They are *family-based* if eligibility is calculated at the family level and/or delivered to a family representative. Both kinds of programs exist within the current system.

Most tax-based programs, such as the Child Tax Credit and the Earned Income Tax Credit (EITC), are family-based.

Because most people file their taxes as a family, family-based programs make means testing relatively easy, but they have disadvantages as well. Not all families share as well as we would hope. Family-based programs can give one family member (usually a man) financial power over their spouse and children. These programs increase the difficulty for a person to leave a spouse (who might be abusive), because they might not be eligible for benefits so long as they are officially part of their spouse's family. It usually takes time and effort to prove one is no longer part of a family, but for many parents and children, those first few weeks and months are the time they have the most acute need and the least available time to fill out paperwork.

Means-Tested
One entailment of a universal and unconditional program is that it is not means-tested; that is, it does not vary with income, wealth, or earnings capacity.

Most traditional welfare programs are not only means-tested but *harshly* means-tested. Some programs require recipients to spend down their wealth and sell their assets to get their means low enough to meet eligibility requirements. Some benefits are completely withdrawn as soon as recipients earn more than a specific amount of money. These conditions can be difficult for people experiencing a sudden need, and they can be exasperating for people facing intermittent periods of need or trying to work their way out of the system.

Like conditional programs, means-tested programs often create a poverty trap by giving beneficiaries an incentive *not* to make any more money unless they can make enough to make up for losing all or most of their benefits.

How UBI Differs from Its Means-Tested Sibling

Means testing doesn't have to be harsh, and it is possible for a means-tested policy to ensure, like UBI, that income doesn't start at zero. A *Basic Income Guarantee* (BIG) is a public policy that ensures everyone's income stays above some nonzero level without any requirement for beneficiaries to work, prove they can't, or meet any other conditions. UBI is the most common term for a BIG without a means test. *Negative Income Tax* (NIT) is the most common term for a BIG with a means test. A NIT's means test is an income test. It does not test other forms of means such as wealth or earnings capacity. Therefore, a NIT has four of the five essential characteristics of UBI.

The difference is simple. A NIT provides a full-size grant to everyone who has no private income, but reduces the grant as their income rises. UBI gives the same grant to everyone regardless of their private income, although it might be combined with an income tax—possibly starting from the first dollar of income.

Unfortunately, none of these terms has become standard. We can say that *Universal Basic Income*, *Unconditional Basic Income*, and *Basic Income* are the most common terms for the non-means-tested form of income guarantee and that *citizen's income*, *citizens dividend*, and *social dividend* are also fairly common. We can say that *Negative Income Tax* is the most common term for the income-tested form of income guarantee. We can say that *Basic Income Guarantee*, *income guarantee*, *guaranteed income*, *guaranteed annual income*, and *minimum income* are common terms for an income guarantee, whether means-tested or not.

But we cannot say any of these are the "right" terms for these concepts. In language, there is no right or wrong, only *standard* and *nonstandard* and *more* or *less common*. Standard terms only appear through usage. Not enough people yet use any of these terms in the same way to make any of them standard. I've defined UBI, NIT, and BIG for the purposes of this book. I've chosen these terms because I think they are widely recognizable, but I warn readers to look carefully at definitions when they see these terms used. Some people use UBI to mean BIG or NIT. Some people use guaranteed income to mean NIT (this use has become increasingly popular in the United States and

Canada recently). Some people use these or similar terms without being clear exactly how they define them.

Now that I've clarified the definitions, we can discuss the substantive differences.

Both UBI and NIT are unconditional in the sense that they reject work requirements. Both are universal, but in different senses. Under UBI, the *payment* is universal: everyone gets it. Under NIT, the *guarantee* is universal: everyone gets it if their income falls below a certain level.

An infinite number of different NIT and UBI plans are possible. By *plan*, I mean the entire scheme by which the policy is introduced, financed, and integrated into the tax-and-transfer system. For every NIT plan, there is an equivalent UBI plan that produces the same distribution after all taxes and transfers are taken into account. The same is not true for every UBI plan: NIT is inherently tied to the income tax, while UBI can be combined with any tax or revenue policy. All three of the example UBI plans discussed ahead tie UBI to an income tax, and so all of them have equivalent NIT plans, but those are just examples.

NIT gradually phases out as income rises, reaching zero at the break-even point. There are no taxes on income until that point. Above the break-even point, positive taxes on income may appear. Although UBI does not phase out like NIT, taxes in an equivalent UBI plan increase at the same rate that NIT decreases so that the break-even point remains the same. Beneficiaries receive the same net subsidy once taxes are subtracted from transfers. The difference is that one program (UBI) requires people both to pay taxes and to receive the grant at the same time, while the other program (NIT) phases out the grant as income rises so that it reaches zero before people begin paying positive taxes.

Because the net amount people receive decreases as income rises under both plans, it is fair to say that NIT is *front-end means-tested* (in the form of declining transfers) while UBI is *back-end means-tested* (in the form of increasing taxes). It is not usually possible for a transfer payment to produce a non-means-tested net benefit for everyone. But as explained ahead, there are advantages to a non-means-tested grant even if its net benefit is effectively back-end means-tested.

NIT appears to be cheaper: it would seem to cost less to give money only to people who need it than to give money to everyone. But NIT and UBI have the same net cost because the only difference between the two plans involves people paying money to themselves. They pay higher taxes under UBI but they also receive a UBI. The two cancel each other out. It costs nothing to give money to yourself. Under a UBI plan, we would give Billionaire Bob a UBI of, say, $12,000 and raise his taxes by $1,012,000, so that his net-tax burden (after all taxes and transfers) rises by $1 million. Under an equivalent NIT plan, we would give Bob nothing and raise his taxes by $1 million even; either way, Bob ends up paying $1 million more in taxes and receiving $1 million less income than he had before. We don't save him any money by choosing either one of the two equivalent plans.

NIT sounds like it should be easier, because it avoids paying and taxing back money from the same people at the same time, but that benefit is very small; both can be accomplished with simple electronic funds transfers. UBI is likely to be easier to administer in ways that are particularly important to people who need it most. Consider the following reasons that UBI is better for net beneficiaries than NIT.

NIT requires continually updated documentation of every person's income every week or every month. Many low-income people cannot produce the documentation they need to prove their eligibility for anything. UBI eliminates the need for low-income people to produce documentation. To get everyone the NIT they are entitled to, the government needs to calculate everyone's household income every week or month (as often as benefits are distributed), including people who hold multiple jobs, who have a sudden loss of income, who suddenly split from a spouse, and so on. The less well-off one is, the harder that is to do.

Imagine fleeing an abusive spouse, taking your children to a shelter, and then having to call some authority to ask for your NIT to be activated because you no longer share an income with the person who legally remains your spouse until you can file for and finalize a divorce. UBI keeps coming to every adult's private account regardless of who they are married to. It would be there for that you and your children in that crisis without any need for you to make a phone call or to prove anything to anyone.

UBI also has a solidarity advantage. *Everyone* gets it—rich, poor, or in between. As an old political saying goes, *benefits exclusively for the poor are exclusively poor benefits*. Social Security, for example, gives benefits to almost every retired person in the United States—regardless of whether they need it or not. Billionaires receive their Social Security when they retire like everyone else. This feature has helped free Social Security recipients from stigma. It has helped keep benefits strong and popular even as the United States cut or eliminated most other social programs. Very few Social Security recipients complain about the complexity of both receiving Social Security benefits and paying taxes on their private retirement income. I expect few will be bothered by both receiving UBI and paying taxes at the same time.

Means testing and categorization (for NIT and many of the programs discussed previously) create the perception of a divide between "taxpayers" and "recipients." In a UBI system, everyone both receives a UBI and pays taxes. Depending on how the overall tax benefit system is structured, UBI beneficiaries pay taxes on whatever private income they might have, their purchases (through a sales or value-added tax), directly or indirectly by land value or real estate taxes on the place they live, and so on.

Net beneficiaries receive more than they pay; net contributors pay more than they receive. Many people's income will fluctuate between net-beneficiary and net-contributor levels from year to year or month to month, and they might not always know for sure which side of the line they're on at a given time. Many people who are net contributors for most of their lives will find that they were net beneficiaries during very crucial points in their life: during education, just after entering the labor force, after being left by their spouse, during a pandemic lockdown, after needing to quit a bad job, and so on.

People in all of these situations are likely to recognize the value of having a UBI always coming in—no forms to fill out, no need to call and request assistance. Under these conditions, it's much harder to vilify beneficiaries. Less animosity is likely to develop as people see that over the course of a lifetime, the vast majority of them benefit in one way or other from the UBI system.

If a politician says, "Let me cut the NIT, and I'll lower your taxes," people who are not receiving the NIT might think they have nothing to lose in this bargain. But if the politician says, "Let me cut your UBI, and I'll lower your taxes even more than you'll lose in the UBI cut," *all citizens*—including net contributors—have something to lose in this bargain. They know their UBI will be cut, but they can't be sure their taxes will be cut as much or more than their UBI. Therefore, UBI is likely to be safer from cuts than NIT.

There is little reason to prefer NIT. The only real advantage for it I can think of is that it avoids the difficulty of explaining the difference between gross and net cost, as chapter 2 explains in more detail (see "The Gross and Net Cost of UBI"). I think it's best to explain that difference and go with the program that most helps people who need it.

How BIG Proposals Differ from Other Policy Reform Proposals

This section discusses how UBI and/or BIG differ from several other policy proposals that have been suggested recently.

In response to the popularity of UBI, people have proposed policies that they call "basic income" but that are actually neither universal nor unconditional. These include basic income for artists, for the unemployed, for single parents, for children leaving foster care, for people leaving prison, and so forth. I've even heard of a "universal basic income for geniuses." None of these is a true Basic Income because none of them are universal or unconditional. UBI is for everyone, which would include people in all of these groups—but if it is targeted at any particular group, it is not a UBI. We could call such programs *targeted basic income*, but that phrase has not so far caught on.

Two forms of targeted basic income are close to UBI: the citizens pension and the child grant. These are similar to UBI because everyone is at one time a child and everyone who lives long enough eventually becomes elderly. With a *citizens pension*, every citizen and/or resident over age X gets $Y, no matter how much they worked when they were younger, no matter whether they are still working, no matter whether or how much other retirement savings they have. Thomas Paine proposed a citizens pension in his pamphlet *Agrarian Justice* in 1797. A *child benefit* can be a one-time or a regular grant to parents for the benefit of their children, again, regardless of income, savings, and so forth. The US has made use of the child grant in the form of the *refundable child tax credit*, especially during the COVID pandemic when it was praised for significantly reducing poverty in the midst of an economic downturn.

A one-time universal income is usually called a *stakeholder grant*. It's usually proposed as a coming-of-age grant to help people get started as they enter adulthood. Instead of giving people a small grant every year, it gives them a very large one at age eighteen or twenty-one. Paine suggested this type of grant along with his citizens pension in *Agrarian Justice*.

Universal basic services (UBS) has recently been proposed as an alternative to UBI. Rather than providing cash, it involves greatly expanded in-kind provision of goods and services. Many UBI supporters also support expanded public services. Some suggest combining UBI and UBS under the name *basic income plus*. But UBI supporters tend to believe that UBS, simply on its own, is merely an extension of the existing model when what is most needed is a new model for reasons discussed throughout this book.

A *participation income* (PI) is similar to UBI, except that it is conditional on some form of recognized participation.[3] Proposals suggest that recognized participation could include holding a private- or public-sector job, taking care of children or others in need, performing volunteer work, being enrolled in education, being too young or old to work, being disabled, being actively looking for but unable to find work, and so on. The idea of PI is usually to leave out two groups: rentiers who live off their assets without working themselves and people who refuse to make any officially recognized contribution no matter how low their income might be. It is, therefore, the closest approximation of UBI possible in a mandatory-participation economy. Chapter 6 discusses the relative merits of UBI and PI (see "Better Than Alternative Reforms").

A guaranteed job, also known as a *federal job guarantee* (FJG) or the *employer of last resort* (ELR), is consistent with the conditional approach to poverty and inequality, but it is a big, sweeping reform that would greatly increase redistribution toward low-income people. Under an FJG, every neighborhood or every small town would have an office that will hire anyone who is willing or able to work at a wage fixed by federal legislation. An FJG would give everyone an effective alternative to private-sector employment.

It would set an effective minimum for wages and working conditions in the private sector because no one would take a private-sector job if it wasn't at least as good as the public job guaranteed to them. It would absorb unemployed labor during recessions but leave labor available to rejoin the private sector whenever attractive jobs become available.[4]

FJG and UBI are not necessarily competitors. They might work well in tandem. But they are often discussed as substitutes. The "Better Than Alternative Reforms" section of chapter 6 discusses the relative merits of FJG as a substitute for UBI.

THE MECHANICS OF UBI

Although chapter 1 provided an in-depth definition of UBI, the concept still remains broad. I have not answered some obvious questions about it, such as how often it would be paid; whether it would vary with the cost of living around the country; what agency would distribute it; whether it would replace existing programs and, if so, which ones; how much it would cost; and how it would be integrated into the existing tax and benefit system.

I don't give definitive answers to these questions because there is no single UBI proposal that unifies the movement for it—nor would it be wise to narrow the movement for UBI behind one proposal. There are dozens or perhaps hundreds of proposals, most of which fit (or nearly fit) the definition of UBI but differ on questions like the ones in the previous paragraph. If and when a UBI eventually comes up for a vote, the particular plan in question is likely to be very different from any of the existing proposals. It will be the outcome of future activism, coalition building, and political negotiation. I could mention some of the attributes I prefer, but this book is about UBI in general, not about any specific version. At this point in the debate, it's better to understand the range of possibilities than to know the specifics of any one proposal. There are good and bad UBI proposals, but it's unwise to believe that only one proposal is good enough to support.

Toward the goal of understanding the range of good UBI plans, this chapter gets into more specific questions, some of which require me to discuss specific UBI proposals, but these proposals are only examples. Many different UBI proposals are possible.

Questions about Possible Specifics

There are always many specific questions to consider about possible UBI plans. This section considers some of the common questions that need to be addressed to come up with a UBI without narrowing the focus to one specific plan.

How Often Would UBI Be Paid?
UBI could be paid at virtually any regular time interval. The closest policy to UBI that exists right now (the Alaska Dividend; see discussion ahead) is paid only once a year.

Most traditional social policies are paid monthly, but I suspect that feature is a holdover from the days when authorities had to cut physical checks. Now that electronic funds transfers are so easy, it would be possible to have the UBI paid weekly, daily, or continuously—in a tiny amount every fraction of a second. I believe smaller, more frequent payments are better help to the people who need UBI most, but a monthly UBI is probably good enough.

Should the Size of the UBI Vary with the Cost of Living around the Country?

This question is tricky. On one hand, we would like to create a decent minimum standard of living everywhere. Varying the UBI with the cost of living is a relatively cheap way to do that. On the other hand, a high cost of living in one area is an economic signal to consider moving to cheaper areas, and there are advantages to leaving those signals in place. A high uniform UBI would leave those signals in place and ensure the decent minimum everywhere, but it would be expensive. Any figure that's just enough to get by in a high-price area would be extremely generous in a low-price area. A low, uniform UBI would be cheaper, but it would not get everyone nationwide up to a decent standard of living.

One option would be to split the difference—partially adjusting UBI to the local cost of living. Another would be to have a uniform federal UBI and leave it up to state and local authorities to supplement it to take into account the local cost of living. Another solution would be to look into the root causes of high prices in some areas and see if changes in rules (such as tax and zoning policies) could reduce prices. A UBI linked to local land value taxes and relaxed zoning restrictions might be part of the solution. No solution is perfect, but we shouldn't let the perfect be the enemy of the good.

What Agency Would Distribute the UBI?

Different proposals suggest different agencies to manage UBI. A new agency could be dedicated only to the UBI, or UBI could be combined with different existing agencies, such as the Internal Revenue Service or the Social Security Administration. This issue is largely a technical one. It should be done by whatever agency can do it with the lowest additional overhead cost.

My guess is that it would work best integrated into the Social Security system. UBI could be the minimum Social Security benefit, so that each citizen received the higher figure of either their UBI or the other Social Security programs they might be eligible for. There would be a great deal of overlap between the UBI and existing Social Security benefits, and the administrative cost would be minimal.

Is UBI Combined with a Flat Income Tax?

Not necessarily; the UBI-flat tax proposal is only one of many proposals that have been suggested. I use it in my examples ahead, but only because it makes the math easy, not because it is necessarily the best proposal. Many people are inherently suspicious of the flat income tax, because many flat tax proposals are regressive.

But there are at least three reasons a flat tax combined with a UBI could be designed as a progressive change. First, it would replace regressive tax deductions with one tax credit: the UBI. Second, the UBI would mean that the effective overall tax rate would be very low for people in the middle to lower end of the income spectrum. Third, the UBI would also make it possible to set a relatively high marginal tax rate (if necessary) without overburdening the lower and middle classes. It would become even more progressive if inheritance and capital gains were treated like any other form of income.

If it were politically possible, my personal preference would be for a flat income tax, probably at a lower rate than in the examples ahead, with the difference made up by other progressive taxes such as a wealth tax, a land tax, a resource-use tax, a pollution tax, a rent tax, capital gains and inheritance taxed as any other income, and so on. Ideally, the government would also purchase fewer of the things lobbyists want to sell. It would charge higher fees for government services provided to corporations by agencies such as the Federal Reserve System, the Federal highway system, the Federal Aviation Administration, the Federal Communications Commission, the Bureau of

Land Management, and so on. If we did these things, a flat income tax rate could be part of a very progressive tax and benefit system, but such a massive reform would have to overcome powerful political resistance.

What Programs (if Any) Will Be Replaced by UBI?
The answer to this question again depends on the specific proposal. To most supporters today, UBI is not about real-locating redistributional funds among low-income people but about greatly expanding our nation's commitment to redistributive policy. But some programs would become redundant and could be replaced once a UBI of sufficient size is introduced. The larger the UBI is, the more programs it can (partially or fully) replace while still helping the people who need it most.

One common misconception about UBI is the belief that it is necessarily part of a grand plan to replace the entire welfare system—including Social Security pensions and disability payments; food stamps; Temporary Assistance for Needy Families (TANF); unemployment insurance; all tax deductions and tax credits, including the EITC and the Child Tax Credit; housing subsidies; public housing; farm subsidies; Medicare; Medicaid; Obamacare; perhaps also the minimum wage; labor- and housing-market regulations; and so on.

These *grand replacement proposals* (for lack of a better term) featured heavily in the BIG discussions in the 1970s

UBI is not about reallo-
cating redistributional
funds among low-
income people but about
greatly expanding our
nation's commitment to
redistributive policy.

in the United States, when replacing the existing system with NIT looked like a grand left-right compromise, simultaneously streamlining and improving the efficiency of the welfare system. In that period, the Nobel-prize winning economist Milton Friedman argued that BIG was *only* worth introducing *if* it replaced the rest of the welfare system.[1]

Grand replacement proposals have continued to appear in various places around the world at various times to this day. But grand replacement proposals have never been the only option for introducing UBI or NIT, nor have they necessarily ever been the most popular kind of proposal within the movement.

Grand replacement proposals have gradually decreased in prominence within the UBI movement in recent decades, possibly because conservatives have become more ambitious about the prospects for cutting the welfare system without replacing it with anything, and because people to both the left and right of center have become more suspicious of the details of grand compromises.

Today, grand replacement proposals appear much less like a left-right compromise than they did in the 1970s. Such proposals appear mostly in libertarian circles. They tend to be discussed minimally, if at all, at the many UBI conferences and activist events held around the world each year.

Most supporters today see UBI as part of an overall progressive strategy of improving social services. They see it neither as a replacement for everything else nor as a way to pare down the social welfare system, even if it would involve the replacement of redundant programs and, therefore, would also significantly simplify the overall social policy system. The point, as most supporters see it, is to expand and improve the system by eliminating all of its gaps. The goal of any good UBI plan is a world in which everyone—young or old, disabled or normally abled, employed or not—has a secure income sufficient to meet their basic needs, no questions asked, no judgment made. If UBI can also help simplify and improve the efficiency of the social policy system, all the better.

How Can You Tell a Good UBI Proposal from a Bad One?
This question becomes important because I've explained that many different UBI proposals—both good and bad—are possible. But I won't be ready to answer it until the end of this chapter.

Three Examples of UBI Plans

This section briefly outlines three simple proposals I use as examples throughout the book. These examples are simplified, both in the sense that they use a flat income tax rather than a combination of many taxes and in the sense that they look at UBI in isolation without explicitly deciding how to integrate it into the existing tax and benefit system. They come from a 2017 study that used 2015 data.[2] I use it here because I don't know of any equivalent study using more recent data.

Different UBI plans are defined by two essential parameters that are chosen by policymakers: the grant level and the marginal tax rate. The *grant level* is simply the size of the UBI. The first example we'll consider here is of a UBI set approximately at the official poverty threshold (more commonly called the *poverty line*)—the income a person or a family needs to escape official poverty. In 2015, the US Census Bureau estimated the poverty line at $12,082 for an individual living alone and $16,337 for a household of one adult and one child (the latter defined as a person under age eighteen).

The *marginal tax rate* is the amount beneficiaries are taxed for each dollar they make in private income. (The UBI itself is not taxed.) It's called *marginal* because it could vary with income—but for simplicity, these proposals assume the marginal tax rate is the same for all levels of income (a "flat" tax).

Example 1 models a UBI plan set at *about* the poverty line because it is virtually impossible to set UBI at *exactly* the poverty line, because UBI is an *individual* grant, and poverty is a *household* concept. Two people living together can live more cheaply (and therefore can escape poverty at a lower income per person) than two people living separately. According to official statistics, children can live more cheaply than adults, and a second child adds fewer expenses than the first child. Official poverty statistics take all these questions of household makeup into account. UBI cannot take them into account because it is uniform, universal, and individual. A UBI set exactly at the poverty line for two people living together would leave single people in poverty. A UBI of exactly the poverty line for a single person living alone would be well above the poverty line for two people living together. UBI proposals tend to split the difference.

Example 1 sets the grant level for adults just below the official 2015 poverty line for single adults, so we can use the round figure of $12,000 per year ($1,000 per month). It sets the grant level for children significantly above the poverty line for the first child, using the round figure of $6,000 per year.

Economist Charles M. A. Clark estimates that it's possible to support a poverty line UBI, and everything else the government is currently doing, with a flat tax rate of less than the current top rate of 37 percent on every dollar a person earns.[3] To make the math easier, example 1 uses a marginal tax rate of 50 percent for all private income for beneficiaries at all levels of income. It stipulates that taxes are levied on *income*, although taxes could instead be levied on spending, wealth, land value, or anything else. This stipulation is also for simplicity: any tax base other than income would make it more difficult to calculate marginal effects on beneficiaries and the net cost of the program.

The *break-even point* is the level of private income at which the taxes a household pays equals the UBI it receives so that the household is neither a net contributor nor a net beneficiary. The break-even point in example 1 is $24,000 for single adults and $36,000 for households with one adult and one child.

Example 2 is a $20,000 grant for adults, $10,000 for children, and the same marginal tax rate of 50 percent. I use this example because official US poverty statistics are very ungenerous. In many places in the United States, people cannot realistically afford rent with $12,000 a year in income. To achieve many of the goals of UBI discussed throughout this book, the more ambitious UBI of $20,000 is probably necessary, but a poverty line UBI is probably a more likely starting point for a politically viable UBI.

Example 3 is a UBI with the original $12,000 grant level and a lower marginal tax rate of 30 percent rather than 50 percent. This example allows me to discuss the effect of the marginal tax rate on the cost of UBI and the possibility of creating a stronger positive work incentive by letting workers keep more of each dollar they receive in the market.[4]

Table 2.1 shows the net transfer to and net income of a single person who receives the UBI in example 1 at four different levels of private income. *Net transfer* is the amount beneficiaries actually get from the government,

Table 2.1 The effect of the UBI plan in example 1 (a grant of $12,000 and a marginal tax rate of 50 percent) on a single individual with no children at four levels of income (all figures in US dollars)

Private income	Grant	Taxes	Net transfer	Net income
0	12,000	0	12,000	12,000
6,000	12,000	3,000	9,000	15,000
12,000	12,000	6,000	6,000	18,000
24,000	12,000	12,000	0	24,000

given that they simultaneously pay taxes and receive a grant. It equals the grant received minus taxes paid. *Net income* is the amount the beneficiary ends up with after all taxes and transfers. It equals private income plus the grant minus taxes. In example 1, the grant is always $12,000, and the tax rate is 50 percent.

If the beneficiary makes $0 of private income, they receive the grant of $12,000 and pay no taxes. Therefore, their net transfer and net income are both $12,000. If their private income rises to $6,000, they continue to receive a grant of $12,000, but they pay $3,000 in taxes, reducing their net transfer to $9,000, and making their net income $15,000. The table continues until the break-even point, at which the individual's $12,000 UBI is equal to the $12,000 they pay in taxes, leaving their net income equal to their private income, $24,000.

Table 2.2 The effect of the UBI in example 1 (a grant of $12,000 and a marginal tax rate of 50 percent) on a family of two adults and two children (all figures in US dollars)

Private income	Grant	Taxes	Net transfer	Net income
0	36,000	0	36,000	36,000
18,000	36,000	9,000	27,000	45,000
36,000	36,000	18,000	18,000	54,000
72,000	36,000	36,000	0	72,000

Table 2.2 shows the effect of the UBI in example 1 on a family of two adults and two children. For this family, the grant level is $36,000 ($12,000 for each adult, $6,000 for each child). It breaks even at $72,000.

The net transfer is important for the next section because it determines the net cost (the real cost) of UBI.

The Gross and Net Cost of UBI

Before the next section discusses *how much* UBI costs, this section first explains something about *how to understand* its cost. That is, only net cost matters. The *net cost* of UBI is the sum of the *net transfers* (the difference between the taxes a beneficiary pays and the grant they receive) to each *net beneficiary* (each person who receives more in benefits than they pay in taxes). The net cost is the only real cost of UBI. The *gross cost* of UBI is a very simple but not at all meaningful concept: the amount of the grant times the number of people who receive it. The gross cost of the UBI in example 1 is $12,000 times the population of adults plus $6,000 times the population of children.

People seldom refer to UBI as a "negative tax" because that invites confusion with the policy proposal *named* Negative Income Tax. But in the generic sense, that's what UBI is. When you give money to the government, that's a *positive tax*. When the government gives you money (without buying anything you're selling), that's a *negative tax*, whether it's called a deduction, credit, grant, or transfer. The only common term we have for a negative tax is a *refundable tax credit*, but that term implies that you get your credit at the end of the year when you calculate your taxes. We could call UBI a "prerefunded tax credit": you get the tax credit every week or month about as frequently as most people get their paychecks. With one being negative and the other being positive, the two partially cancel each other out. Only the difference between the tax and the credit matter to you or to anyone.

Confusion exists because although UBI works like a refundable tax credit, it is aimed at goals similar to redistributive spending programs. People therefore want to calculate its "cost" in the way we calculate other redistributive programs rather than in the way we calculate the cost of other deductions and tax credits.

Although the Office of Management and Budget estimates the cost of *special* (i.e., targeted) exclusions, deductions, and credits, we do not think of *regular* tax deductions as "costing" anything. If we did, they would cost trillions of dollars per year. For example, the US government gives everyone a standard (i.e., minimum) tax deduction of $13,850—and much more to people who itemize. This means that the first $13,850 of everyone's income is untaxed. The cost of not taxing that amount of income depends on what the tax rate would have been.

If we think of taxing that amount of income at the rate of the lowest bracket (10 percent), then the minimum deduction is equivalent to an individual tax credit of $1,385, and its gross cost is $1,385 multiplied by the population (333 million people), making $461 billion. If we think of that amount of income being taxed at the rate of the highest bracket (37 percent), the equivalent individual credit is $5124.50, making the gross cost $1.7 *trillion*.

That cost is purely notional, so we simply ignore it altogether. We need to do the same with the portion of each individual's UBI that is canceled out by the taxes they pay. This means we have to focus on the *net* amount people receive after subtracting their UBI from their taxes, because the rest they effectively pay to themselves. It does not cost or benefit you to pay something to yourself, nor does it benefit or burden anyone else.

The net cost issue requires careful explanation because it is specific to UBI, extremely important, and sometimes difficult to grasp. Remember that UBI is universal, in cash, and regular. Because it is *universal*, everyone receives it, even net contributors. Because it is also *in cash*, people both pay and receive the *same thing* (money). Because it is also *regular*, people both pay and receive the same thing *at the same time*.

Most other transfer programs pay money to people who are not also paying the taxes associated with it. For example, almost no one simultaneously pays income taxes and receives unemployment insurance, TANF, disability insurance, Medicaid, and so on. People pay the vast majority of their Social Security taxes years before they receive Social Security benefits. The net issue is small, negligible, or nonexistent for all these policies, but it is extremely significant to UBI.

About half of US transfer payments are healthcare related, and many of these do involve the same people both paying taxes and receiving associated benefits at the same time, but they pay *cash* and receive *care*. The most relevant cost of health care is not its redistributive effect but the cost of converting cash that people would otherwise use to buy something else into healthcare, using government's tax and spending powers to shift production from other goods to healthcare. The real cost of any policy is goods for goods, but we measure the cost of goods in dollars.

Therefore, the gross cost of healthcare spending is relevant in a way that the gross cost of UBI is not.

UBI is fundamentally different both from nonuniversal and from in-kind transfers because it takes and gives the same thing at the same time. Therefore, to understand the costs and benefits of UBI, you need to understand that its gross cost is meaningless and that its net cost is what matters.[5]

The Cost of UBI

This section presents simple, back-of-the-envelope estimates of the net cost of the three example UBI plans described earlier, leaving the question of how to pay that cost for the "Options for Paying for UBI" section. The information in this section is based on the previously mentioned study using 2015 data.[6] The dollar figures will all have risen slightly since the time of that study because of inflation, but the figures in terms for percentage of gross domestic product (GDP) will all have fallen slightly because of economic growth.

Key findings about the cost of example 1 include the following (all dollar figures in 2015 dollars):

• The net cost of a roughly poverty line UBI ($12,000 per adult, $6,000 per child is 2.95 percent of GDP per year, or $539 billion.

- This UBI plan would drop the official poverty rate from 13.5 percent to about 0 percent, eliminating poverty for 43.1 million people (including 14.5 million children).

- This UBI costs less than 25 percent of current US entitlement spending and less than 15 percent of overall federal spending.

- Sixty-one million households, 48.9 percent of all US households, are net beneficiaries of this plan, making it an effective wage subsidy (or tax cut) for tens of millions of working families.

- The average net beneficiary family includes about two people making about $27,000 per year. The family's net benefit from the UBI would be nearly $9,000, raising their income to almost $36,000.

- The net cost of this UBI is less than 16 percent of its often-mentioned but not very meaningful gross cost.

One reason UBI's net cost is so much smaller than its gross cost is obvious: under this UBI plan, less than half of citizens are net beneficiaries; everyone else effectively pays their entire UBI to themselves. Another reason is just as important but less obvious: most net beneficiaries pay a significant portion of their own UBIs to themselves. Net beneficiaries receive $1.375 trillion in UBI grants but pay $840 billion in UBI-related taxes. That is, the average net beneficiary pays 61.1 percent of the gross cost of their UBI through taxes.

The taxes paid by net beneficiaries do not interfere with UBI's ability to do what it is designed to do: end the threat of poverty and reduce economic inequality. The average household in the lowest income range of $0–$5000 receives nearly $20,000 in net subsidies, bringing it from very deep poverty (well below the official poverty line) to a position safely above the official poverty line. The average net beneficiary family receives a net subsidy of about $9,000, which raises their income to more than twice the official poverty line. This finding shows that although UBI is unconditional, it is also an effective subsidy for working families.

The key findings of the study for example 2 are as follows (all dollar figures in 2015 dollars):

• The net cost of a UBI of $20,000 per adult and $10,000 per child with a 50 percent marginal tax rate is $1.816 trillion per year.

• The cost of the $20,000 UBI plan is about 32 percent of its gross cost ($5.692 trillion).

• The cost of the $20,000 UBI plan is about 85 percent of current entitlement spending, about 49 percent of total federal spending, and less than 10 percent of GDP.

The key findings of the study for example 3 are as follows (all dollar figures in 2015 dollars):

• The net cost of a UBI of $12,000 per adult and $6,000 per child with a marginal tax rate of 35 percent is $901 billion per year.

• The net cost of this UBI plan is less than half of current entitlement spending and only 4.95 percent of GDP.

• Lowering the marginal tax rate from 50 percent to 35 percent spreads the net benefits of the UBI program to more of the middle class. Nearly 70 percent of citizens would be net beneficiaries.

The biggest difficulty of implementing UBI is not its cost but working it into the existing tax and transfer system. Implementing a UBI without making any other changes would create very high marginal tax rates for some net beneficiaries; the marginal tax rate from the examples discussed here would be added to the marginal tax rates people face now. In addition, many existing targeted transfers create high marginal tax rates at some point on the lower end of the income distribution. Unfortunately, the tax and transfer system in the US is so complicated that it is hard to estimate how many households will be affected, to what extent, and over what range of income.

The 2015 study did not explicitly examine how to resolve the marginal tax rate issue, but there are at least three indications that it might be relatively inexpensive to solve:

1. Although this UBI scheme introduced without other changes creates high *marginal* tax rates for some net beneficiaries, the *total taxes* paid by all net beneficiaries decreases—often significantly.

2. To the extent that the marginal tax rate issue is caused by the phaseout of transfers targeted at low-income households, it is a problem with the current system rather than with UBI. Moving toward a simpler UBI model can help to fix it.

3. Average households in the bottom 60 percent of the income distribution currently receive more in transfers than they pay in income taxes, which indicates at least some potential for reducing marginal tax rates by replacing other transfers with UBI.

It would be best to introduce UBI along with other changes in the tax code so that recipients faced a marginal tax rate (the portion of each dollar of income paid in income taxes) of 50 percent or lower. Doing so would increase the cost of the program. But a more sophisticated study taking that factor into account will not change the basic result that the real cost of a UBI is far less than its gross cost and amounts to a few percent of GDP per year.

Perhaps the most striking feature of the three examples presented in this chapter is how inexpensive they are. Considering what even the cheapest of them can do, $539 billion is a bargain. At a cost of only 2.95 percent of GDP, 14 percent of total federal spending, and 25 percent of current transfer payments, the United States could eliminate poverty under the official definition.

This study was limited to the US, but countries with similar per capita income and similar tax and benefit systems can expect a similar UBI scheme to cost a similar percentage of their GDP.[7]

Do We Even Need to Consider "How to Pay for" UBI?

Before we discuss options for paying for UBI, we need to consider whether it is even necessary to consider that question. One school of economic thought, modern monetary theory (MMT), stresses the truism that taxes don't actually "finance" spending. Every time the government spends, it creates money out of thin air. It doesn't need to go get the money to spend by taxing or borrowing. However, the government does need to *resource* spending. That is, it needs to make sure goods are available to buy so that government spending doesn't increase inflation. Very often, considerable fiscal space is available, and so the government can buy goods without taking any action to resource or finance spending. However, how much fiscal space is available depends on many fluctuating factors. In general, fiscal space is larger during economic recessions and smaller during economic booms.

If MMT is correct, particularly targeted policies—such as an FJG—could take up the available fiscal space without sparking inflation. Some fiscal space is available now, and UBI could take up some of that space, but there are at least five reasons not to assume UBI can be resourced entirely out of the available fiscal space.

First, available fiscal space is highly variable depending on the state of our complex macroeconomy. UBI is not targeted to using up fiscal space the way an FJG is. If the goal of UBI is to make sure everyone has enough to live on, we wouldn't want it to vary in size with the availability of fiscal space.

Second, if we introduce a livable UBI with no new taxes whatsoever, its gross cost and net cost would be the same, and we would be pumping $2 to $6 trillion worth of inflationary pressure into a $20 trillion economy every year, far outstripping any reasonable estimate of the available fiscal space during any nonrecession year.

Third, if we introduce UBI with at least enough new taxes to make the net cost relevant, it is far less likely to exceed the available fiscal space, and if it does exceed the available space, it will do so by a far lower amount than if we introduce it with no new taxes whatsoever.

Fourth, maintaining UBI is not the only thing the government could do with that fiscal space. If the government ever adopts MMT, the available fiscal space will be quickly taken up by programs targeted to take up the available fiscal space.

Fifth and finally, fiscal space is not a limit on the amount of spending that is possible. If the government wants to expand public sector resource use more than the amount that would take up the available fiscal space, it needs to discourage private sector spending to free up the necessary resources. Taxes are the government's primary tool to free up the resources necessary to make new spending possible without creating inflation. Taxes are not the only tool, and taxes don't need to match one-to-one with spending, but a one-to-one ratio isn't a bad approximation given that we don't know the state of the macroeconomy in advance and that we are assuming other policies will be targeted to take up the available fiscal space.

The most important thing to understand about paying for UBI is that the resources are available. The "Cost of UBI" section showed that a UBI at about the poverty line costs about 3 percent of GDP and that a UBI of $20,000 per year (about 167 percent of the poverty line) costs about 10 percent of GDP. The US GDP has *doubled* in the last forty years or so. Almost all of those gains have gone to people in the top 1 or 2 percent of the income distribution.

Even if none of the consumption of UBI net beneficiaries comes from expanding our currently underutilized economic capacity, it is physically possible for people at the top of the income distribution to reduce their purchases enough to free up the resources necessary to produce the goods that net beneficiaries would consume. Anything that is physically possible is financially feasible. UBI is therefore financially feasible.

In this context, taxes and regulations need to be understood as tools to reallocate resources away from people at the top of the income distribution toward people in the middle and bottom. With that understood, I use the common term *to finance spending* rather than the MMT term *to resource spending*, even though it's about freeing up resources rather than getting money.

Options for Paying for UBI

Now that we have a ballpark idea of how much UBI costs, we can more realistically consider how to pay that cost—or (in MMT terminology) how to resource the goods that UBI net beneficiaries will consume.

The most obvious strategy is to replace programs that are already doing some of the things UBI does. Your first thought is probably of other policies aimed at low-income people, but remember that UBI is also a tax credit. It can therefore replace other tax credits, tax deductions, and tax loopholes. According to Bloomberg Tax, special tax expenditures amount to 6.8 percent of GDP each year, making it possible to finance a large chunk of the net cost of UBI by replacing tax expenditures.[8] People with larger incomes get the uniform UBI payment instead of their corporate and personal income tax deductions, and their marginal tax rates might not need to increase at all.

As mentioned earlier, one estimate indicates that a flat tax of less than 37 percent on all income could finance everything the government is currently doing *and* a UBI at about the poverty line. It's tempting to say "look no further," but there are lot of other good options. If we add other taxes or expenditure reductions to the mix, we could reduce the income tax rate or increase the size of the UBI.

If the UBI system is going to be partly financed by replacing other redistributive programs, it should be done on a "hold harmless" basis: ensuring everyone living on the margins is at least as well-off under the UBI system as they were before. Any good UBI plan is about redistribution from the people with the highest income and wealth to people with less or with nothing at all. It is not about rearranging benefits between different groups of low-income people. Therefore, this chapter looks for savings from redistributive programs only by cutting up to the point that would leave recipients no worse off under UBI than under the previous system.

For example, rather than replacing Social Security (or parts of if), UBI could be integrated into it, as the minimum benefit in a system of "Social Security for All," so that UBI would be synonymous with the first $12,000 or $20,000 of Social Security or Supplemental Security Income (SSI) benefits—significantly increasing benefits for many current recipients and having no effect on people who currently receive more than $12,000 per year in Social Security benefits. It could of course be done in such a way that everyone currently receiving Social Security becomes a little better off than they are now while still saving money via integration.

Social Security paid about $743 billion in cash benefits in 2015 (the year of the study). If UBI integration saved a quarter of that total ($185 billion), that would be a very good start toward paying for the $539 billion net cost of the $12,000 UBI. The integration of the $20,000 UBI into Social Security would save most of that budget, because only a small portion of beneficiaries receive more than $20,000 per year in individual benefits. And so the savings would take a big chunk out of the $1.8 trillion cost of that proposal. Other cash assistance programs, such as unemployment insurance and TANF, could also be subsumed into this Social Security for All system, increasing the savings.

In addition, some—perhaps many—nonredistributive programs could be cut to support UBI. For one example, the United States military budget is twice as large as Russia's and China's budgets combined, and at least some of it is designed to satisfy lobbyists more than to meet strategic need as assessed by military leaders. For another, the Federal Reserve Board could raise much more net revenue if it required banks to pay market rates for the insurance protection it provides them.

But of course, although it is possible to raise a great deal of revenue by cutting other spending, any effort to do so is controversial and involves entering a conflict with the political interests that support that spending. UBI supporters should choose their battles wisely, and they should not be afraid to propose higher taxes. The enormous increase in US inequality over the last forty to fifty years indicates that higher taxes on upper-income people are economically feasible and strongly desirable.

Sales taxes, or their more sophisticated cousin, value-added taxes (VATs), are an option. On the face of it, a VAT is regressive because poor people spend more of their income on consumption than rich people, who save and invest a large portion of it instead. But who pays a VAT depends on what portion of it businesses are able to pass on to consumers in the form of higher prices. Some estimates indicate that businesses end up paying more than half of VATs in the form of lost profits because they are unable to pass on more than 45 percent of the cost to consumers. If so, a VAT might be an effective way to tax business profits. A VAT would be far less regressive if it were combined with a UBI, and some Republicans, Libertarians, and at least one Democrat (Andrew Yang, who ran for the Democratic nomination for president in 2020) have suggested such a link.

One excellent option is to tax rentier income. A *rentier* is someone who makes money because they own stuff, rather than because they do stuff. We like to pretend that all income comes from "work," but human effort is only one factor of production. Anything we use to make other goods is a factor of production. The big money in the world isn't made from doing anything but from owning the nonhuman factors of production, which are usually categorized as either capital or land (including all natural resources). *Capital* (confusingly) refers both to the physical goods used to produce things and to the money used to buy or rent the land, labor, and physical capital needed to produce things. To make the term just a little more confusing, the term *human capital* is sometimes used to refer to skilled labor.

People who receive income from land or capital are called rentiers. They might also work (managing their assets or doing an unrelated job), but like UBI beneficiaries, *they do not have to work if they don't want to*. The income generated by a factor of production goes to the person who owns it. The owners of land and physical capital get paid whether or not they have worked, managed, or contributed any effort to production.

One way to find out how much of the return on an asset goes to the manager and how much to the owner is to look at university endowments that are managed by outside firms, because their records are public. According to Thomas Piketty, Harvard University makes 12 percent on its endowment of more than $50 billion. It pays a rate of 0.5 percent to the firms that manage its assets.[9] That leaves Harvard with a rate of 11.5 percent (more than 95.8 percent of the total return) in pure rentier income. Owning assets pays twenty-four times as much as managing them.

A tax on assets can actually increase the incentive for owners to keep the asset working. For example, in the absence of land taxes, investors often buy real estate and let it sit, hoping its value will increase over time. With a land value tax, it becomes expensive to hold land unless you make sure it's working and generating income to pay the taxes. Therefore, if we tax the rental value of factors of production, we actually increase owners' incentive to keep those assets working rather than leave them idle for speculation or use them for personal consumption.

If we shift taxes onto the stuff people own and away from the things they do, we can raise enormous amounts of money, greatly reduce inequality in asset ownership, and still give people the same incentive to do the productive stuff we want them to do. Therefore, taxes targeted at rentier income (land value taxes, natural resource taxes, wealth taxes, banking taxes, etc.) are economically efficient ways to reduce inequality.

Wealth taxes are another way to tax rentiers. They are a little trickier than land and natural resource taxes, but worth using. A *wealth tax* takes a small percentage, perhaps a half a percent or as much as perhaps 2 percent, of the total value of an individual's wealth each year. So long as the wealth tax rate is below the normal rate of return on assets, the holder can afford to pay the tax out of the returns on their wealth, and it gives them an incentive to keep their wealth in productive activities.

Another way to tax the wealth of rentiers is to tax the transfer and growth of wealth by treating capital gains and inheritance like any other income. Right now, people whose income comes from work pay higher tax rates than people whose income comes from capital gains and inheritance, which effectively means the wealthy pay lower tax rates than everyone else.

Pollution taxes make people pay for the harm they do to the environment. If these taxes are high enough, they are an extremely effective way to discourage pollution and environmental degradation, and revenues from these taxes can be used to support a UBI. If the high resource and pollution taxes we need to discourage environmental harms create excessive contractionary pressure, the solution is easy: recycle the excess revenue with a UBI, stimulating the economy while giving everyone an incentive to switch their consumption to more environmentally friendly goods and services. An environment tax–linked UBI effectively makes environmentally damaging consumption relatively more expensive and environmentally friendly consumption relatively less expensive, so that it changes our consumption toward the more environmentally friendly goods without discouraging overall economic activity.

The environment tax–linked UBI rewards below-average polluters by making them net beneficiaries of the tax-benefit combination, and at the same time, it penalizes above-average polluters by making them net contributors into the system. This feature is desirable from an equity perspective, a policy prospective, and a political perspective.

Critics of this link point to the truism that if such taxes effectively reduce environmental harm, the revenue they raise will eventually fall, but that's a good thing. If and when environmentally damaging activities becomes so rare that we can no longer raise much revenue from taxes designed to discourage them, there are plenty of other taxes we can use to counteract the inflationary pressure of UBI.

This discussion shows that there are more than enough available taxes to counteract the inflationary pressure that

UBI creates. What mix of taxes we should use is largely a strategic political question. We should consider two principles of taxation suggested by Adam Smith 250 years ago: they should be based on the ability to pay and collected by the method that makes it easiest for people to comply.

Our tax system does nearly the opposite today: it taxes low-income people at higher rates than high-income people and makes tax compliance extremely difficult for everyone—possibly because large accounting firms make big campaign contributions to keep it that way. A curb on the power of the so-called donor class could greatly expand prospects for UBI and the taxes necessary to make it work.

I suggest a mix of small simple taxes and fees: large pollution and rentier taxes, a small wealth tax, a small financial transaction tax, fees for services the government provides to corporations (such as the banking system), the elimination of all tax deductions and tax credits other than the UBI, and capital gains and inheritance taxed like all other income. If we do all that, income and sales (or value-added) tax rates could be reasonably low.

Unfortunately, if we cannot eliminate or reduce the control that the donor class has over our politics, the question is not what the optimal mix of taxes is but which tax reforms we can get through given the likely resistance of powerful campaign contributors.

It is possible that increased taxes will have a negative effect on the amount of time and effort people put into productive moneymaking activities. But there are at least four good reasons to think this problem is not insurmountable and perhaps not terribly significant. First, many of the taxes I've suggested are directed at rentier income. The more taxation is shifted toward the rental value of things people own and away from the things people do, the less negative effect it has on productive activity. There is enormous room to shift in this direction, if we can gather the political power to do so.

Second, even taxes on the things people do are not terribly well correlated with the amount they produce. The US had its highest income tax rates during the period between World War II and about the mid-1970s. This was also the period in which the US had its highest productivity growth rates. Some of the highest-taxed countries (Finland, Norway, Iceland, etc.) also have some of the highest economic output.

Third, every year, economic growth gives people a greater marginal incentive to work. That positive incentive counteracts the negative incentive effect of taxes on labor. According to the US Federal Reserve Board of St. Louis, US GDP today (the early 2020s) is double what it was in the early 1980s and four times what it was in the early 1950s. This means that an hour spent working at the average income gives the worker four times as much added consumption as it did in the early 1950s. Therefore, a 75 percent tax rate would give people the same consumption incentive to work an extra hour as they had in the early 1950s—even if taxes back then had been zero. People worked pretty hard in the 1950s, and taxes were higher than than they are now. Therefore, we can expect a tax rate of 30 percent, 40 percent, or 50 percent to leave people with a very significant incentive to work in terms of the added consumption they can expect from an additional hour or day or week of work.

Fourth, maybe we're working too hard. Maybe we should enjoy a greater portion of the benefits of the economic growth we have experienced over the past century in the form of more leisure time rather than in the form of increased consumption. Giving people the incentive to take and enjoy that leisure time is not a bad thing.

How Can You Tell a Good UBI Proposal from a Bad One?

There are many factors to consider in evaluating a UBI plan. Some are technical, such as whether it is realistic, sustainable, and sensibly integrated into the existing tax and benefit system—for example, without creating excessive marginal tax rates over some range of income.

Many of the benefits discussed throughout this book require a UBI large enough to live on, but livability is not all there is to a good proposal: a smaller UBI can be an important step in the right direction.

If you agree that UBI should be part of a greater commitment to using redistributive policy to increase equality, decrease poverty, and improve the well-being and freedom of the people who have the least, then you'll need to compare the net gains and losses for the people who need UBI most.

Look at the programs being replaced, the changes to the tax system, the marginal tax rates, and the size of the UBI. Consider how the overall cost and benefits of the change are distributed. Compare the net benefit for people in the middle to low end of the income distribution under the existing and proposed systems. If all or most of them are better off and if any additional taxes and fees that might be necessary to counteract the program's inflationary pressure are paid by the people who are most able to pay and if they are collected in ways that make it easy to comply, then it's a progressive change. If instead substantial numbers of people at the low end are worse off and people at the high end find themselves with a lower overall tax bill, then the proposal is yet another regressive change in an economy that has experienced a series of regressive changes over the last half century.

It is possible for a grand replacement proposal to pass that test, but to determine if one does, consider whether it includes the replacement of tax credits and deductions that primarily benefit the rich. If it involves replacing only programs aimed at low- and middle-income people, it's probably a regressive change.

Many grand replacement proposals promise to spend "all" the money saved by canceling existing programs on UBI. But do they count the amount they spend in UBI in gross or net terms? If they count it in terms of net cost, it probably will be a progressive change. But if they count in terms of gross cost, as little as one-third or even one-sixth of the net benefit is likely to go to people in the lower half of the income distribution. A large portion of the funds will be funneled into a tax rebate for upper-income people. A plan like that will almost certainly be regressive.

You have to look at net cost and net benefits to answer all of these questions. Gross cost simply is not relevant.

THE HISTORY OF UBI AND RELATED POLICIES

Support for UBI has grown so rapidly over the past few years that people might think the idea appeared out of nowhere. In fact, the idea has roots going back hundreds or even thousands of years, and activists have been floating similar ideas with gradually increasing frequency for more than a century.[1]

Since 1900, BIG has experienced three distinct waves of support, each larger than the last: a small one between 1910 and 1940, followed by a down period in the 1940s and 1950s. A second and larger wave of support happened in the 1960s and 1970s, followed by another down period in most countries through about 2010. BIG's third, most international, and by far largest wave of support so far began to take off in the early 2010s, and it has increased every year since then.

Support for UBI has grown so rapidly over the past few years that people might think the idea appeared out of nowhere.

Any effort to identify waves of something as complex as international political support is necessarily a simplification, and waves in one place don't always correspond with waves in other places, but simplification does not need to be perfect to be useful. This chapter presents UBI history in this narrative form to make it possible to draw lessons from when and where the discussion tends to have come and gone.

Before the First Wave

We could trace the beginnings of UBI into prehistory, because many have observed that "prehistoric" (in the sense of nonliterate) societies had two ways of doing things that might be considered forms of unconditional income.

First, nomadic, hunting and gathering societies of less than sixty people have often been observed to treat all land as *commons*, meaning that everyone can forage on the land but no one can own it. A similar right to use land has existed in many small-scale agrarian communities right up to the enclosure movement, which was not complete in Europe until the twentieth century and is not complete around the world today. The connection between common land and UBI is that both institutions allow every individual to have access to the resources they need to survive without conditions imposed by others.

Second, most observed small-scale, nomadic, hunter-gatherer societies had strong obligations to share what they had with others. If someone camping with the group found more food than they and their immediate family could eat in one meal, they had to share it with everyone in the camp, including people who rarely or never brought back food for the community. The food shared around camp could be seen as a "basic" income.

The modern definition of UBI stipulates the grant must be in cash, and because small-scale hunter-gatherer or agrarian communities do not have cash economies, they do not have UBIs. But these practices show how the values that motivate much of the modern UBI movement are not new to politics but have been recognized and practiced for a very long time.

Some writers trace the beginning of UBI history to ancient Athens, which used revenue from a city-owned mine to support a small cash income for Athenian citizens. This institution sounds like a UBI, except that the meaning of *citizen* was very different in ancient Athens. Citizens were a small, elite portion of the population. Noncitizens, such as slaves, women, and free noncitizen males, were the bulk of the population and virtually all of its labor force. A UBI for the elite is no UBI at all.

Proposals that begin to fit the modern definition of UBI begin in the 1790s with two writers, Thomas Paine and Thomas Spence. Paine's famous pamphlet *Agrarian*

Justice argued that because private ownership of the land had deprived people of the right to hunt, gather, fish, or farm on their own accord, they were owed compensation out of taxes on land rents. He suggested this compensation should be paid in the form of a large cash grant at maturity plus a regular cash pension at retirement age. That amounts to a stakeholder grant plus a citizens pension: nearly, but not quite, a UBI.

From a similar starting point, Spence carried the argument through to a full UBI, calling for higher taxes on land and a regular, unconditional cash income for everyone. If anyone can be said to be the "inventor" of UBI, it is Thomas Spence, but his proposal remained obscure, and the idea had to be reinvented many times before it became widely known.

Joseph Charlier, a Belgian utopian socialist author, reinvented the idea of UBI in 1848, suggesting the socialization of rent, with the proceeds to be redistributed in the form of a UBI.

Henry George, a late nineteenth-century economist, set out to solve the problem of persistent poverty despite economic progress. He proposed taxing land value at the highest sustainable rate and using the proceeds for public purposes. At one point, he suggested that part of the proceeds could be distributed in cash to all citizens, but UBI was never a central part of his proposal.

BIG proposals remained sparse until the early 1900s.[2]

The First Wave

By the early twentieth century, enough people were discussing BIG to constitute its first wave—or at least its first ripple—of support. The idea was still new enough that most advocates had little knowledge of each other, and they all tended to give their versions of the program a different name.

In the United Kingdom, Bertrand Russell and Virginia Woolf both praised the idea in their writings without naming it. In 1918, Dennis and E. Mabel Milner started the short-lived State Bonus League, which briefly attempted to get a conversation started with pamphlets and other publications, including what was probably the first full-length book on UBI: Dennis Milner's 1920 publication *Higher Production by a Bonus on National Output*.[3]

Several economists and social policy analysts, especially in Britain, discussed UBI, often under the name *social dividend*, in the 1930s and early 1940s. These included James Meade (economist and later Nobel laureate), Juliet Rhys-Williams (writer and politician), Abba Lerner (economist), Friedrich Von Hayek (economist and later Nobel laureate), Oskar Lange (economist), and G. D. H. Cole (political theorist, economist, and historian). It was apparently Cole who coined the term *basic Income* in 1935, although that term did not become standard for more than fifty years.

Major C. H. Douglas (a British engineer) included UBI under the name *national dividend* in a wider package of proposed reforms he called *social credit*. His ideas were most prominent in Canada, where the Social Credit Party held power in two western provinces on and off between 1935 and 1991, but the party abandoned support for Douglas's proposed dividend not long after it first took power.

In 1934, Louisiana senator Huey Long debuted a Basic Income plan he called Share Our Wealth. He seems to have come up with the idea on his own; there is no evidence that he was influenced by the ideas spreading around the United Kingdom in those years. Long's plan might have served as the basis for a presidential run in 1936 had he not been assassinated in 1935.

Although some of these early advocates were highly respected people, they were unable to get any form of BIG onto the legislative agenda in this era. As World War II drew to a close, most Western democracies built up their welfare systems on a conditional model, typified by the British government's famous Beveridge Report, which recommended fighting poverty, unemployment, and income inequality with a greatly expanded welfare system based on the conditional model. Discussion of BIG largely fell out of mainstream political discussion for nearly two decades.[4]

The Second Wave

Discussion of BIG was kept alive between the first and second waves largely by economists who increasingly portrayed it as an interesting theoretical alternative to existing social policies.

During the second wave, the phrases *income guarantee* and *guaranteed income* were often used without indicating whether the guarantee was an NIT or a UBI. When specified, it was most often an NIT. However, the second wave was extremely important in directing international attention toward the idea of creating a world in which everyone would have an income above poverty level.

The second wave took off in the early to mid-1960s, when at least three groups in the United States and Canada separately started promoting the idea at about the same time. First, feminists and welfare rights activists, including Martin Luther King Jr., mobilized people frustrated by inadequate and often demeaning conditional programs. The feminist and welfare rights movements for BIG were closely tied together because there was widespread belief that existing welfare programs were inadequate, punitive, and too closely tied to the belief that "typical" families were "headed" by a "male breadwinner" with a "housewife." Feminists led a large grassroots effort to replace US welfare programs with BIG, and it became an official demand of the British Women's Liberation Movement by the 1970s.[5]

Second, futurists such as Robert Theobald and Buckminster Fuller saw a guaranteed income as a way to protect workers from disruptions to the labor market caused by the computer revolution. This effort foreshadowed the automation argument for UBI in the 2010s, but it dropped off considerably in the 1980s and 1990s.

Third, several Nobel Prize–winning economists—including James Tobin, James Meade, Herbert Simon, James Buchannan, F. A. Hayek, and Milton Friedman—and many other prominent economists began arguing that a guaranteed income would represent a more effective approach to poverty than existing policies. To them, BIG would have been an attempt to simplify and streamline the welfare system while also making it more comprehensive. The interest from economists made BIG a hot topic among policy wonks in Washington and Ottawa.

The mainstream media started paying attention to NIT around the time Lyndon Johnson declared War on Poverty. Politicians and policy advisors began to take up the idea. The Canadian government released several favorable reports on guaranteed annual income in the 1970s. For a short time, many people saw some kind of BIG as inevitable and as the next step in social policy: a compromise that everyone could live with. People on the left viewed it as the final piece of the welfare system—a policy that would fill in the remaining cracks. Centrists, conservatives, and people from the burgeoning libertarian movement saw it as a way to make the social safety net more cost-effective and less intrusive.

In 1971, the US House of Representatives overwhelmingly passed a bill introducing a watered-down version of

NIT. It missed becoming law by only ten votes in the Senate. The next year, presidential nominees from both major parties endorsed a variety of similar proposals: Richard Nixon supported the watered-down NIT, and George McGovern briefly proposed a genuine UBI. The similarity of the two nominees' positions probably made BIG less of an issue in the campaign than it would have been if one of them had opposed it.

Although Nixon won the 1972 election, BIG never got another vote. It died partly because it had no groundswell of support outside the politically marginalized welfare rights movement. Its proponents in Congress made little effort to sell the proposal to the public at large. Many prominent guaranteed income supporters viewed Nixon's version with skepticism, seeing it as too small with too many conditions to fit the model. In the absence of a wider movement for BIG, politicians paid little or no political cost for letting Nixon's plan die and letting the idea fade from public discussion.

Although the second wave was most visible in the United States and Canada, the discussion spilled over into Europe, even as the second wave waned in North America. A high-level government report in France focused on NIT in 1973. At about the same time, James Meade and others managed to draw attention to the idea in the United Kingdom. In 1977, Politieke Pariji Radicalen, a small party in the Netherlands, became the first party with representation in parliament to endorse UBI. The next year, Niels I.

Meyer's book *Revolt from the Centre* launched a substantial wave of support in Denmark.

People often look back on the second wave of the BIG movement as a lost opportunity because no country introduced a full UBI or NIT, but the second wave had some major successes. The United States and Canada conducted the world's first BIG implementation trials (see chapter 4). The United States created or expanded several programs that can be seen as small steps in the direction of BIG, including food stamps, the EITC, and the Child Tax Credit. All these programs provide income supplements to low-income people. Although they have restrictions and conditions that UBI and NIT don't, they represent steps toward BIG because they have fewer conditions than most traditional social policies and because they were proposed or expanded as compromise responses to the guaranteed income movement.

In 1982, the State of Alaska introduced the Permanent Fund Dividend (PFD). As I'll explain in chapter 5, the PFD provides yearly dividends, varying usually between $1,000 and $2,000 per year to Alaska residents. Despite being very small, Alaska's PFD is the closest program yet to meeting BIEN's definition of UBI—falling short only by requiring people to fill out a form to verify that they meet the residency requirement.

Not only did these policies help a lot of people, but their success also provides evidence that can help to push social programs slowly in the direction of universality. But by the late 1970s and early 1980s, politicians such as Ronald Reagan and Margaret Thatcher dramatically changed the conversation. They successfully vilified virtually all welfare recipients as frauds, no matter how well they might have satisfied programs' need-based criteria. As a result, many people stopped talking about how to expand or improve the welfare system and started talking about whether and how much to cut it. In response, the left largely went on the defensive. Any suggestion that the existing system might be replaced by something better could at that time be seen as lending support to people who wanted to cut existing programs and replace them with nothing.

In 1980, the United States and Canada canceled the last of their implementation trials. Canada stopped analyzing the data that it had spent years and millions of dollars collecting. For the next thirty years, with a few notable exceptions, mainstream politics in most countries included virtually no discussion of BIG.[6]

Between the Waves

The 1980s, 1990s, and 2000s were downtime for BIG in world politics, but there were significant exceptions, when proposals briefly gathered attention in one place or another. These exceptions and the growth of academic interest in

UBI were extremely important to building what became the third wave of the BIG movement. In 1982, a British parliamentary committee considered a UBI proposal. National waves of support happened in the Netherlands, Denmark, and postapartheid South Africa at various times. But for the most part, discussion of UBI took place outside the political mainstream.

Proposals continued to come out in various circles, but they were more easily ignored in this period. For example, Leonard Greene, an aviation expert and successful entrepreneur, wrote two books and sponsored a demonstration project in which he gave a small UBI to several families, but he received little, if any, media response.[7] When I had the pleasure of meeting him, he described his ten-year-old son's reaction to UBI, "So what you're saying is that income doesn't have to start at zero." I've used that phrase ever since.

One place the UBI discussion grew steadily in this period was in academic journals. In 1984, a group of Britons, led mostly by academics, formed the world's first national UBI network, the Basic Income Research Group (now the Citizen's Basic Income Trust). In 1986, a group of academic researchers established a group that was initially called the Basic Income European Network (BIEN). Philippe Van Parijs (a Belgian philosopher) and Guy Standing (a British economist) were the most active leaders of BIEN for the first twenty or twenty-five years of its existence.

From the founding of BIEN to the present, UBI, rather than NIT, has dominated the BIG movement. However, in the last few years, the NIT model has come back. In some countries, the BIG discussion is dominated by NIT, usually under other names, such as guaranteed income.

The academic debate grew substantially between the mid-1980s and the 2000s, especially in the fields of politics, philosophy, and sociology. By the mid-2000s, national groups existed in at least two dozen countries, including the United States, where the US Basic Income Guarantee (USBIG) Network had been established in December 1999. Because so many UBI networks around the world wanted BIEN affiliation, the network changed its name to Basic Income Earth Network in 2004. Yet UBI stayed mostly outside the political mainstream.

I became interested in UBI as a high school student in 1980, just as the second wave of discussion was dying down. I started writing about it professionally after finishing graduate school in 1996, when the idea seemed hopelessly out of the mainstream. For those of us taking part in UBI events in the late 1990s and early 2000s, it felt less like a movement and more like a discussion group.

Even the activist contingent within BIEN and other networks concentrated more on discussion than action, believing (probably correctly) that they had to increase public awareness before they could gather the critical mass of support needed to make political action viable.

Isolation from mainstream politics distracted supporters from how much their movement was growing. But as supporters would learn in retrospect, they were helping to lay the groundwork for a takeoff.[8]

The Third Wave

Interest in UBI has grown enormously since 2010. The discussion crossed over into the mainstream international media by the mid-2010s. In some places, the crossover began earlier. Those of us who were volunteering at BIEN's Basic Income News service noticed a substantial increase in media attention in late 2011 and early 2012, and media attention has grown steadily since. It is impossible to attribute the third wave of the UBI movement to any single source. It is the confluence of many widely dispersed actions and events, which I will try to sketch here as well as I can.

The financial meltdown of 2008, the subsequent Great Recession, and the Arab Spring sparked a new climate of activism. Public attention turned to poverty, unemployment, and inequality. UBI supporters suddenly had a much more welcoming environment for activism.

By 2008, a national wave of UBI support had begun to swell in Germany. Prominent people from across the political spectrum all began to push different UBI proposals in very public ways. That year, UBI activists in Germany, Switzerland, and Austria attracted the critical mass necessary for effective UBI activism and jointly organized the first International Basic Income Week. This event has taken place every year since and has spread around the world, now including actions as far away as Australia and South America.

In 2008, the Namibian Basic Income Grant Coalition, funded mostly by private donations from the Lutheran Church, began a two-year pilot, giving a small Basic Income to every resident of a rural Namibian village. This project coincided with a smaller one in Brazil and was followed by a much larger one in India in 2010 (both also largely or entirely funded by private donations). These trials attracted substantial media attention both locally and internationally. They helped inspire the privately and publicly funded experiments later conducted around the world.

Just as the Indian experiment faded from the headlines, European activists introduced UBI to the European mainstream media by pushing two citizens' initiatives, one in Switzerland and one in the European Union, both of which attracted hundreds of thousands of signatures. The EU initiative recruited across Europe and collected signatures from every EU member state. The Swiss initiative collected enough signatures to trigger a national vote, which was held in 2015. Although neither initiative ultimately passed, they both built an infrastructure for UBI activism across Europe and attracted enormous international media attention, which in turn sparked additional activity and attracted more support.

At about this time, journalists around the world started paying attention to UBI, greatly increasing its visibility. By 2015, a third wave was visible to people who were paying attention, and all subsequent activism for UBI owes something to the cumulative results of the actions up to that point.

However, the chain of activism building on activism was only one of many sources of growth in the UBI movement. One of the movement's most important strengths is its diversity: support comes from many different places and from people who do not usually work together, follow similar strategies, or adhere to similar ideologies.

By the time the UBI experiment was underway in Namibia, economists and sociologists had already begun reassessing the results of the 1970s NIT experiments in the United States and Canada, bringing renewed press attention to BIG and helping to spark new interest in the idea.

Another source of momentum for UBI came from developing countries that had been streamlining and easing the conditions of eligibility for redistributive programs by creating what are now known as *conditional cash transfers* (CCTs). Although these programs were conditional, the results from *easing* conditions were so positive that they significantly bolstered support for further steps toward UBI, not only in lesser-developed countries of the Global South but all around the world. At least one CCT program, Brazil's Bolsa Familia, inspired by the senator and UBI advocate Eduardo Suplicy, was introduced explicitly as a step toward UBI.

The third wave of the UBI movement is more identifiably left of center than the second wave, which involved many people who portrayed BIG as a compromise between left and right. But some right-of-center support has boosted the movement as well. For example, a group of philosophers and economists calling themselves Bleeding Heart Libertarians wrote a significant amount of pro-UBI literature in the 2010s.

Mirroring the futurism discourse of the 1960s, new attention to the automation of labor and the related precariousness of employment brought many new adherents to UBI. As unemployment reached new highs during the Great Recession and job openings lagged behind the overall economic recovery, many people, especially in high-tech industries in the United States, began to worry that the pace of automation was threatening large segments of the labor force with high unemployment, low wages, and gig-economy precariousness. Labor leaders, activists, academics, and tech entrepreneurs have all proposed UBI in response, making automation-related labor market changes one of the prime drivers of recent interest in UBI, especially in the United States. Some entrepreneurs, such as Chris Hughes of Facebook and the late Götz Werner of the German drugstore chain DM, have put their money where their mouth is, supporting UBI research, activism, and experimentation, giving an unquestionable boost to the movement.

Another way technology has affected the UBI debate is through *cryptocurrencies* (privately issued, all-electronic mediums of exchange). Some people see cryptocurrency as a way to bypass central banks entirely and provide users with a UBI in the newly created currency.

Environmentalism has also played a major role in the growth of interest in UBI. Two of the most popular proposals for combating climate change are the tax-and-dividend and cap-and-dividend strategies, both of which involve setting a price on carbon emissions and distributing the revenue to all citizens—thereby creating at least a small UBI. Some environmentalists see UBI as a way to counteract the depletion of resources by giving people a way out of the cycle of work and consumption. These kinds of proposals have received support from both Republicans and Democrats.

Growing interest in UBI, and to some extent tech industry money, have inspired a new round of UBI and UBI-related pilot projects in Finland, Kenya, Canada, the Netherlands, Germany, the United States, and many other places. UBI experiments are both a product and a driver of the current wave of support for UBI. This new round is characterized mostly by many small experiments rather than the few large experiments of the 1970s. Part of the reason is that many of the contemporary experiments are privately financed and therefore have to work on more limited budgets.

One exception is GiveDirectly's enormous project in Kenya. This nonprofit has raised enough funds to finance a UBI of seventy-five cents per day for twenty thousand people for twelve years, in an area where many people live on a dollar per day or less. When complete, this study will be the largest and longest UBI experiment ever conducted.

Between 2017 and 2020, UBI support got a large boost from Andrew Yang's campaign for president of the United States. He was the first major-party candidate to endorse UBI since 1972, and the first ever to make UBI the centerpiece of their platform. For a political outsider, Yang did extremely well, qualifying for debates and recruiting a large network of supporters. Partly inspired by Yang, many candidates for lower offices also endorsed UBI in 2020 and 2022.

US activism for UBI took off in October 2019, when activists in New York organized a UBI march from Harlem to the South Bronx. Hundreds of people participated in the New York march, while thirty cities around the world joined in with their own marches. The march was so successful that organizers decided to make it an annual event.

The 2022 march took place on September 24 at the climax of Basic Income Week.

Just as Yang suspended his campaign in 2020, UBI got yet another boost from an unexpected source. The COVID-19 outbreak and the related economic meltdown gave impetus for a temporary, emergency UBI. Suddenly mainstream politicians across the world were discussing UBI.

UBI was particularly well suited to the COVID situation. It functions as a cushion for people who are unable to work either because of social distancing or because of the economic downturn, and at the very same time it functions as a bonus for the essential workers asked to remain on the job during a pandemic. In both ways, it helps reduce the severity of the recession by stimulating the economy from the bottom up. To some extent, these policies represented politicians catching up with activists who had been calling for quantitative easing for the people (rather than for bankers) since the start of the Great Recession in 2009.

As late as perhaps 2015, it remained unclear whether the third wave would match the size and reach of the second. By 2019, the answer was obvious: grassroots support and international media attention are more extensive than ever. The third wave represents the first truly global wave of UBI support. The first two did not extend much beyond the United States, Canada, and the United Kingdom, but the third wave involves major campaigns on all inhabited continents.[9]

The Pattern

This look at the ups and downs of the UBI movement shows that UBI has tended to enter the mainstream conversation at times when people were concerned with and open to new approaches to address inequality, poverty, and unemployment. UBI has tended to recede from the mainstream conversation when public attention turned to other issues, or when other ways of addressing inequality became dominant. The first wave subsided when policymakers settled on the attempt to build a comprehensive welfare system on the conditional model. The second wave subsided (at least in the United States and Canada) not in the prosperous economy of the mid-1980s but in the troubling times of the late 1970s, when right-wing politicians convinced large numbers of people that redistributive programs should be cut instead of improved.

The biggest danger to the third wave appears to be growing nationalism. If nationalist politicians can convince enough voters to blame immigrants and foreign competition for growing inequality, they can effectively distract people from mobilizing around better social policies. But, chapter 8 will later argue, the prospects for UBI remain encouraging.

UBI has tended to enter the mainstream conversation at times when people were concerned with and open to new approaches to address inequality, poverty, and unemployment.

EVIDENCE ABOUT UBI'S EFFECTS

Because UBI in its full form does not yet exist, all sources of empirical evidence about its effects have serious limitations, but at least three kinds of evidence are useful. First, because UBI has a direct effect on poverty and equality, evidence about the effects of reduced poverty and increased equality is crucial. Second, researchers can extrapolate from evidence about the effects of other redistributive policies that are or have been in place around the world. Third, the findings of the many, diverse UBI-related experiments, pilots, and demonstration projects—let's call them *trials*—are also useful, but their value relative to the other two sources of evidence is often exaggerated. This chapter discusses these three kinds of evidence.[1]

Evidence about Poverty and Inequality

UBI directly addresses poverty and economic inequality. If the grant level is set above the poverty line, it mathematically eliminates poverty. By giving a grant to everyone and taxing those who have more, it greatly reduces inequality. Because UBI directly affects these two issues, evidence about their costs provides evidence about the benefits of UBI.

According to the Poor People's Campaign, 250,000 Americans die from the complications of poverty and inequality every year. Child poverty alone costs the United States more than $1 trillion per year in lost economic productivity, lost health, increased crime, and incarceration. Hunger costs $178.8 billion per year in health care expenses and educational outcomes. These figures ignore nonmonetary human costs. How much money is the death of a human being worth? What is the monetary value of building a society in which no child is forced by financial necessity to experience periods of hunger, malnutrition, and homelessness?

The Poor People's Campaign also provides evidence of how hunger, food insecurity, homelessness, and housing insecurity scar children in ways that are costly to them and to society as a whole throughout their future lives. Children who grow up in poverty complete two fewer years of schooling than average for all children, they work less, and they end up in worse health throughout their lives. Children and teenagers who experience poverty and homelessness are more vulnerable to physical maltreatment and sexual exploitation. Infant and childhood mortality are closely correlated to poverty.

An extensive cross-country study of inequality by Richard Wilkinson and Kate Pickett found that inequality is costly to society as a whole, not just to people at the bottom of the distribution.[2] Inequality is associated with reduced life expectancy, poorer educational outcomes, higher crime, higher incidences of mental health problems, increased drug abuse, greater obesity, more unhappy children, increased bullying behavior, more social distrust, more suspicion, and reduced economic growth. In more equal societies, people throughout the income distribution tend to have greater trust in their fellow citizens.

According to Wilkinson and Pickett, the reason inequality affects everyone is that the more a society is divided into haves and have-nots, the more mental, physical, and economic capital everyone has to expend to protect or improve their position. Every child grows up with more stress and fear about their future. Everyone spends more on positional goods that help them move up or maintain their place in the hierarchy. These goods don't just include showy luxuries; they also include social necessities, such as entrance into the top schools at all levels of education. In societies with low levels of inequality and in which good quality education is available to all, parents don't stress over getting their children into an elite elementary school.

Of course, people at the top do get some benefits from living in a highly inequal society, but at some point, the additional benefits come down to easier and easier access to more and more luxuries, no amount of which can make up for the physical and psychic cost of living in a fearful and antagonistic society.

Wilkinson and Pickett also find that the countries with the highest equality of outcome (places like Norway, Sweden, and Japan) tend to have the highest economic mobility. America's self-perception as the land of opportunity has not been true for a half century or more—if it ever was. A child born poor in the United States has a lower chance of dying rich than a child born poor in almost any other wealthy democratic country.

At least one of the causal connections between equality of outcome and equality of opportunity is obvious: the outcome for one generation is the starting point of the next. Low-income children in our highly unequal society often grow up with greater food and housing insecurity in communities in which they are unlikely to make the social connections that can help them move ahead. Highly unequal societies waste an enormous amount of talent.[3]

This discussion shows that problems directly addressed by UBI are enormously costly. UBI will at least partly reduce these costs. Nevertheless, it's reasonable to ask for evidence of whether UBI is a particularly good way to address these problems.

One answer is provided by basic economic theory, which predicts that UBI is an economically efficient transfer. It is a lump-sum grant: everyone gets it regardless of whatever else they do. Therefore, they have no incentive to change their behavior *to get the grant*. They might change their behavior *because they have the grant*, but this does not involve the efficiency loss of expending time and effort to get the grant. A person with more money can afford to work fewer hours. But people have no need to reduce their work hours to keep the grant the way people have incentives to stay out of employment to maintain their unemployment insurance or to keep their income low enough to maintain their eligibility for housing assistance, food stamps, TANF, and so on.

Most of the taxes usually proposed to support UBI do involve incentives to work less, such as income and value-added taxes. But there are some opportunities to support UBI with efficient taxes that target rent-generating assets and rent-seeking activities. Therefore, economic theory gives reason to believe that a well-structured UBI plan can reduce poverty and inequality with minimal side effects, as was argued in chapter 2.

The following two sections look at empirical evidence indicating that UBI is a particularly good way to address poverty and inequality.

Economic theory gives reason to believe that a well-structured UBI plan can reduce poverty and inequality with minimal side effects.

Evidence from Related Policies

Cross-country comparisons show that direct policy interventions can significantly reduce or eliminate problems associated with poverty and inequality. The Nordic countries (Denmark, Finland, Iceland, Norway, and Sweden) have some of the most aggressive government policies aimed at reducing poverty and inequality and some of the highest levels of well-being and greatest economic mobility observed in the world.

Between the 1930s and the 1970s, the United States had relatively active policies aimed at reducing poverty and inequality. It experienced significant reductions in poverty and significant improvements in health, well-being, longevity, and economic mobility. Since about 1980, the United States government has gradually reduced its commitment to fighting poverty and inequality, and it has seen a significant slowing—perhaps an outright reversal—of the trends toward increased equality and improved quality of life observed in the mid-twentieth century. The ability of policy to affect trends like these is confirmed by similar experiences throughout wealthy democratic countries.

Existing policies that are relatively similar to UBI have proven particularly effective in reducing poverty and inequality. In the last twenty to thirty years, many low- and middle-income countries, especially in Africa, Latin America, and South Asia, have introduced CCTs. Obviously, the conditionality of these programs means that they are not UBIs, but they represent a significant step in that direction because their conditions are designed to be very easy to fulfill. For example, they might involve keeping children in school or getting them vaccinated.[4]

A cross-country study of CCTs by Armando Barrientos, David Hulme, and Joseph Hanlon found that the more generous the CCT and the easier the conditions are to fulfill, the more the CCT improves the well-being of recipient families. The logical limit of a movement in that direction would be the introduction of the highest sustainable UBI. The authors of the study make it clear that they draw a similar conclusion in the title of their book, *Just Give Money to the Poor*.[5]

A study in *American Sociological Review* found results in wealthier nations that were consistent with the results of CCTs in less wealthy nations. The more universal the government's welfare programs, the more successful the country tends to be at reducing poverty. My coauthors and I reach similar conclusions in our two books about the Alaska Dividend (see chapter 5).[6]

In another example, the Eastern Band of Cherokee Indians has been distributing dividends from the band's casino revenue for nearly twenty years. Researchers studying the dividend have found that children who were lifted out of poverty by it were less likely to commit crimes or abuse drugs and alcohol and that behavioral problems among them declined by 40 percent.[7]

Although oil and casino dividends might be the closest existing US policies to UBI, other policies, such as Social Security, the EITC, the Child Tax Credit, the COVID stimulus payments made to individuals, and, to a lesser extent, unemployment insurance, all move toward reduced conditionality in cash-based benefits, and they have proven to be the most effective at decreasing poverty, inequality, and insecurity.

A study in the Netherlands showed that every dollar spent on eliminating homelessness returned two to three times as much in savings on social services, police, and courts. A Utah program providing free homes for the homeless on an unconditional basis found savings of 150 percent of the cost. These savings are in terms of tax cost only. They would be far larger if they included overall benefit to society.[8]

Many different empirical studies connect unconditional cash grants with decreased child mortality, crime, teenage pregnancy, and malnutrition, as well as with increased school attendance, school performance, economic growth, and gender equality. Evidence from these studies indicates that unconditional cash grants are more effective at improving quality of life than in-kind and conditional grants. Policies that require officials to figure out what people need and then get it for them build in more expense and more opportunities for error than policies that give people cash and let them buy what they need.[9]

In-kind and/or conditional policies seem to be premised on the twin beliefs that low-income people do not know what they need and that the people administering the program know so much better that they can overcome the additional expense of researching needs and delivering goods rather than cash. The greater empirical effectiveness of cash grants indicates that low-income people know their own needs better than administrators.

From this evidence, we should learn that the government is not good at making decisions for disadvantaged people, but it is good at giving them cash if it respects them enough to do so.

Evidence from UBI-Related Trials

Trials can help fill in some of the gaps from the two main sources of evidence, but because it is impossible to approximate all relevant attributes of a permanent, national UBI in a short-term, small-scale experiment, trials inevitably end up testing something other than a true UBI. For example, because trials can't levy taxes, they end up either testing NIT or exaggerating the net benefit of the UBI.[10]

Importantly, trials cannot observe *community effects*; that is, they cannot observe how the market or society as a whole will react when everyone in the country has a UBI. Trials divide participants into an *experimental group* that receives the grant and a *control group* that does not, but trials are only able to observe the initial reactions of the people in these two groups at the individual level. Trials cannot observe all the feedback that would occur throughout the community if a UBI were introduced. For example, trials can observe whether the experimental group worked less than the control group, but they cannot observe whether employers would respond by raising wages or improving work conditions. Trials can observe how one child performs in school when her family is free from poverty, but not how much more she might be affected when all children in her school or her nation are free from poverty. To get a fuller picture, researchers have to estimate the market responses to UBI, filling in the story of how they believe the market will react by drawing on theory, evidence from other sources, and computer simulations.

For these reasons, the interpretation of the findings of UBI-related trials requires just as much theory as the effort to extrapolate from similar policies. Unfortunately, it is extremely difficult if not impossible for people reporting on UBI trials to communicate their findings in a way that is both simple enough for nonspecialists to read and understand in the time they have and cautious enough to head off misunderstanding, misuse, oversimplification, and spin. Very often, reports of experimental findings simply state the raw comparisons between the control and experimental groups as if community effects did not exist.

My book *A Critical Analysis of Basic Income Experiments* explains the difficulty of communicating what experiments can and cannot show in short form.[11] This book presents the task of summing up essential knowledge from dozens of experiments conducted over more than fifty years in a short form that helps first-time readers avoid potential pitfalls. This task is especially difficult considering that a central point of the book is that no list of caveats can eliminate all the inherent difficulties in understanding.

Therefore, the best advice I can give is that people should look at experimental evidence cautiously and skeptically. Avoid the common tendency to exaggerate the importance of UBI trials relative to other forms of evidence. Try to understand not only the findings themselves but also the theory of how the effects of a real UBI are likely to differ. Be aware of the various ways people with different points of view interpret and spin those numbers. Often, the best use of experimental evidence is to see whether it confirms—that is, points in the same direction—or contradicts evidence from other sources.

So far, there have been two waves of UBI-related trials. The first involved five large-scale NIT experiments conducted by the US and Canadian governments between 1968 and 1980. The second began with a Basic Income project in Namibia (2008–2009), continued with another in India (2011–2013), and has grown ever since with more and more trials being conducted all over the world. The current wave involves many more projects that tend to be smaller and more diverse. They also tend to focus more on UBI than on NIT and to rely more heavily on private funding than the first round of studies.

The next two subsections summarize evidence from UBI trials. The first one examines the direct effects of UBI on the quality of life of net recipients. The second subsection then examines one potential effect that plays a particularly important role in the UBI debate: the effect UBI has on the amount of time low-income people spend making money.

Quality of Life

Experimental findings for quality-of-life indicators are relatively easy to understand and difficult to spin either way. The biggest danger is overinterpretation. Because trials cannot observe community effects, they can't answer more specific questions, such as whether a UBI of $X causes a Y-amount change in quality-of-life indicator Z, but they can indicate the direction of change, such as whether UBI tends to increase or decrease indicator Z.

Results for quality-of-life indicators from the first round of experiments were substantial and encouraging. According to a summary by Robert Levine and colleagues, researchers found large, positive effects on school attendance rates, number of years of study, and test scores of children and young adults in the worst-off families receiving NIT. In one study, high school graduation rates rose by 30 percent. Some found an increase in adults going on to continuing education. All of these outcomes are extremely difficult to achieve with direct intervention in education in low-income communities. It appears that ensuring children grow up free from poverty is one (perhaps the most) important way to help children learn.[12]

Positive effects were also found for homeownership, childhood nutrition, and food consumption. Some studies found reduced domestic abuse, reduced psychiatric emergencies, and reduced incidents of low-birth-weight babies. The birth-weight finding is extremely important because low birth weight is a sign of a very serious health deficit that can affect children throughout their lives. Canada's contribution to the first round of NIT experiments was the Manitoba Basic Annual Income Experiment, or Mincome. It was particularly interesting because it included a "saturation site" in which all residents of the town of Dauphin, Manitoba, were eligible for a poverty-line NIT. Economist Evelyn Forget described the site as "the town with no poverty" and found significant positive results, including reductions in hospitalizations (especially for mental health and accidents), improved school performance, increased number of years of schooling, decreased domestic violence, and decreased incidence of teenage and college-age pregnancies.[13] These findings confirm the predictions about UBI's effectiveness that earlier sections drew from evidence about poverty and inequality.

One Mincome finding specific to BIG was that the lack of pressure to find another job helped people land the right job. David Calnitsky drew on qualitative participant accounts from Mincome to show that its design largely freed beneficiaries from social stigma. According to Calnitsky, "The social meaning of Mincome was sufficiently powerful that even participants with particularly negative attitudes toward government assistance felt able to collect Mincome payments without a sense of contradiction."[14]

The second round of BIG trials began twenty-eight years after the first round concluded. The first of the new round of UBI trials was the Namibian Basic Income Grant Pilot Project (2008–2010). Like Mincome, it was a saturation study in which a grant of about US$16 per month was given to each resident of a village of just under one thousand people in rural Namibia.

Researchers found extremely promising results, including significant decreases in household poverty, child malnutrition, underweight children, household debt, crime, and so on. Results also included significant increases in savings rates, economic activity, access to medication and healthcare, school attendance, and household savings. Many beneficiaries used the money to purchase livestock, pay school fees, and repair their homes. Researchers observed increases in labor market participation and small business activity. Women were empowered both economically and socially, making them better able to escape abusive relationships and avoid prostitution. Researchers observed that people had a greater sense of hope, greater sense of community spirit, and increased social cooperation. Predicted effects of increased alcohol consumption did not come true: people receiving the UBI drank the same amount as typical Namibians.[15]

Shortly after the conclusion of the Namibian project, twin projects took place in India, one in Madhya Pradesh and the other in tribal villages from 2011 to 2013. Researchers found similarly promising results, including significant decreases in illness, child labor, household indebtedness, anxiety, stunted growth, and freedom from the cycle of debt and predatory lending. Results also included significant improvements in food consumption, food security, nutrition, medical treatment, school attendance, school performance, household savings, and on-the-job productivity. Many farmers invested their UBI payments into their farms. Some beneficiaries changed occupations or moved into self-employment.[16]

Since 2017, the US-based nonprofit organization GiveDirectly has been conducting a major UBI project involving more than ten thousand people across dozens of villages in Kenya. The project is planned to last for at least twelve years and may become permanent if donations continue. Although the main motivation of it is to help people using a UBI-inspired model, GiveDirectly is taking advantage of the opportunity for study. This makes Give-Directly the world's largest and longest-lasting UBI experiment yet attempted. The organization is simultaneously conducting smaller studies in other parts of the world.

Results from GiveDirectly's research will trickle out for years. So far, its website reports that recipients experience increased food security, improved psychological well-being, decreased domestic abuse, increased ability to pay for medical expenses, and increased investment in housing and income-generating assets (such as livestock). As in the Namibian study, GiveDirectly reports no increased alcohol consumption—a particularly important issue in the African political context.

A 2019 project in Stockton, California, the Stockton Economic Empowerment Demonstration (SEED), was the first of now more than one hundred municipal-level UBI pilots being conducted in the United States. SEED gave 125 randomly selected residents $500 per month for twenty-four months. Researchers reported that UBI beneficiaries showed signs of enhanced well-being and improved physical and mental health and were better able to take risks.

Many other experiments are underway or in the planning or proposal stages around the world. New results will be coming out for a long time.

One obvious pattern arises from these experimental results: they all seem to confirm or extend the encouraging observations made from the studies of poverty, inequality, and related policies. This correlation is so regular that Bru Laín labels it the *redundant effect*, writing, "If economic poverty is what we intend to solve with Basic Income experiments, then unconditionally granting people money must reduce or substantially mitigate problems associated with its lack."[17] In this sense, the role of UBI experiments is to provide more and more confirmation of the observations made from poverty and inequality data—or more and more evidence that UBI works as promised. But Laín's statement also points to two limitations of experiments, both of which I discuss in my book on UBI experiments.[18]

First, as noted earlier, experiments cannot tell us *how much* a UBI of a given size will improve various quality-of-life indicators. The final outcome for any factor depends on complicated community effects that play out differently when everyone in the nation has a permanent UBI than when a few randomly selected individuals have a temporary, UBI-like grant.

Second, most UBI experiments are unable to differentiate between the *size* and *type* of benefit examined in the experiment. The UBI grant being studied is usually substantially more generous than existing redistributional programs that members of the control group continue to receive. Therefore, experiments can show that an unconditional grant of that size can help people in those ways, but it cannot show whether it does so *better* than an equal amount of money spent on other programs. To test UBI against just one other type of redistributive program could nearly double the cost of an already expensive project.

Only two studies I know of have been able to test UBI against other policies of a similar size. First, because Give-Directly works with some of the poorest populations in the world, its budget goes much farther. GiveDirectly's researchers have been able to compare various types of aid, and they have consistently found that direct, unconditional cash grants perform better than other forms of aid. Second, Finland tested a UBI-like grant equal in size to the country's existing unemployment insurance benefit. Participants in the experimental group reported improved well-being, reduced stress, greater trust in other people and in social institutions, and greater confidence in their ability to find work and make a positive impact.

Both theory and experience predict these results are likely to hold in the wider context. Economic theory stresses the efficiency advantages of a lump-sum, unconditional grant that is streamlined but generous, with little overhead cost and without counterproductive substitution effects. Experience with existing policies indicates that more generosity and less conditionality lead to better outcomes and lower cost.[19] All of this indicates that a livable UBI will have an extremely positive effect on the quality of life of disadvantaged people.

Time Spent Making Money

UBI-related trials can help shed light on the question of how UBI will affect the amount of time people spend "working," which in this context means "time spent making money" either in paid labor or in self-employment.[20] The time people spend in productive non-moneymaking activities (e.g., caring for children, the elderly, or other people in need) seldom counts as "work" in these discussions. People put non-moneymaking work into a different category that draws far less political attention. To the extent that it does draw attention in this context, it's often labeled as a bad thing because the unpaid work might take time away from moneymaking activity. Therefore, the discussion of the effect of UBI on "work effort" or "labor market participation" is really about time spent making money.

UBI experiments draw a great deal of attention to the issue of labor time because it is very easy to observe the number of hours worked by the experimental group (receiving UBI) and the control group (not receiving it). But this attention is problematic for two reasons.

First, the difference between the number of hours worked by the experimental and control groups in a trial is a poor predictor of the effect of an actual UBI on the long-term behavior of people in the national labor market.

Actual market outcomes depend on the interaction of employers and workers, but that interaction is a community effect that isn't observable in a small-scale experiment with a randomly selected sample of people. Economic theory predicts that employers would respond to a decline in labor supply by offering higher wages and better working conditions, partly or perhaps fully reversing any initial decline in hours worked. If this happens when UBI is introduced, it will reduce the cost of the program and enhance its ability to fight poverty and inequality. UBI-related trials often report only raw comparisons between the control and experimental groups, ignoring the predictable difference between experimental and actual outcomes.[21]

Second, the labor supply issue is the Rorschach test of the UBI debate. Widely divergent beliefs exist about what to look for in the results:

• Some UBI supporters focus on the connection between sustainability and affordability: as long as the decline in labor supply isn't large enough to make the program impossible to maintain, UBI is, in an important sense, affordable.

• Some opponents portray *any* negative labor supply effect as a reason to reject UBI entirely, no matter how small it might be and no matter what other benefits UBI might have.

- Some supporters concede that a negative labor supply effect is bad, but argue either that it can be accepted (within limits) given the other benefits of UBI or that UBI has no such effect.

- Some supporters believe (as I do) that a decrease in labor supply within the sustainable range is a good thing because middle- and low-income people are working too many hours right now and because it indicates that UBI gives disadvantaged people more effective control over their working lives and more power to command better wages and working conditions.

Researchers in the first round of experiments in the 1960s and 1970s focused on sustainability, and they were pleased to find the labor market effect was clearly within the affordable range even for beneficiaries who received an NIT of 150 percent of the US poverty line. All UBI-related trials since then have confirmed the finding that labor market effects are within the sustainable range.

Unfortunately, when the bulk of the findings of the first round of NIT experiments were reported, the focus on sustainability played into the hands of people who portrayed *any* negative labor supply response as a reason to entirely reject the idea. The mere fact that the group receiving NIT averaged fewer work hours per week than the control group dominated the discussion and was usually taken as reason to conclude that BIG failed the test. Although empowerment for the disadvantaged was one of the motivations for the BIG movement of the 1960s, the idea was largely, if not completely, absent from the mainstream media's response to the findings of the NIT experiments in the late 1970s.

Five recent UBI-related projects in Namibia (2008–2009), India (2011–2013), Kenya (2014–present), Finland (2017–2018), and Stockton, California (2019–2020), found a positive labor supply response. That is, participants receiving the grant worked as much as or, in some studies, *more than* the comparison group of people not receiving the grant.

The difference in results is mostly attributable to two factors: the size of the grant tested and the group targeted by the study. Across the various studies, researchers have tested grants as low as fifty cents per day and as high as 150 percent of the US poverty line. In all or most trials, the sample of people studied is drawn from a target group that is not meant to represent the nation as a whole. The studies in Namibia, India, Kenya, and Stockton targeted some of the poorest people in their respective countries with very small grants.

These studies confirm something that poverty experts have long known: extreme poverty often prevents people from working. Many people don't work as much as they would like because they can't afford a car or bus fare to get to the place their job was offered, because they can't afford the right clothing to look presentable, because they are too busy trying to find the food and shelter they need to get them through the next day. Therefore, we should expect that a small grant given to extremely low-income people who are not already working full time would increase their labor market participation.

The four studies in Namibia, India, Kenya, and Stockton all confirm that prediction. That is an important and encouraging result, but it should not be taken as representative of what is likely to happen if the UBI were larger and available to the population as a whole. One important way to mislead people in favor of UBI would be to tout such results as some kind of proof that no UBI scheme makes people any less likely to accept employment. Those results were specific to the parameters of the test, and the parameters tested were very different from the type of UBI scheme most supporters would like to see.

The Finnish experiment also found a slight increase in labor supply, but it was probably for a different reason. The target group was limited to people who were already collecting long-term unemployment insurance, and the grant level was equal in size to the unemployment insurance benefit. The UBI allowed recipients to move in and out of employment without penalty, while the unemployment insurance program required people to remain unemployed to maintain eligibility. That is, the unemployment insurance benefit has a poverty trap, and UBI does not.

This difference probably explains the slight increase in employment associated with UBI in the Finnish study. The small size of the increase might indicate that the poverty trap was not a major cause of long-term unemployment in Finland, but it might be attributable to the short duration of the two-year study.

The 1970s NIT experiments tended to target families whose incomes were slightly above or below the poverty line, and most of the grants offered were significantly more generous than existing redistributive programs.[22] The US studies left out people with high incomes because researchers reasonably assumed that the NIT would have little effect on their behavior. Most US studies also left out people who were already out of the labor force (students, families with incomes coming entirely from existing redistributional programs, etc.) because if many of them remained out of the labor force, including them would greatly increase the cost of the study. This strategy allowed researchers to estimate the labor supply curve with minimal cost. The likely nonresponse of the groups left out of the study could be filled in by theory.

It was a scientifically sound decision, but it was politically troublesome because it targeted the people who were most likely to respond by working less. One study using computer simulations to account for targeting, labor demand response, and other factors found that the reduction in labor time would be only about one-third of the reduction observed in an experiment in Gary, Indiana, at the time (1.6 percent rather than 4.5 percent). Nevertheless, the political response discussed previously was based almost entirely on the raw comparison of the control and experimental groups, with no consideration of how targeting affected the numbers or what the findings indicated about how the national labor market was likely to respond to a real, long-term, national UBI.

Most critics simply reacted to the finding that the labor supply response was negative with no consideration that the finding was small, fully expected, and well within the sustainable range. The discussion in the mainstream media ignored the finding that no one in any of the studies dropped out of the labor force or that the labor supply response was mostly attributable to people taking more time between jobs to find the right job.

The discussion ignored that the largest declines in "work effort" came from mothers who spent more time taking care of children and by students who stayed in school longer—declines that might not have involved any drop in "work" in the broader sense of the term. The effort people put into non-moneymaking activities and the economic and social value of those activities counted for nothing.[23]

Today's discussion seems to be less vulnerable to anti-UBI spin than the first round of experiments. Many of the people involved in the debate seem better informed about the likely labor market effects, and some people have stressed the empowering feature of a grant that allows people to refuse bad jobs. Awareness of how those discussions have played out in the past will be extremely useful to anyone discussing the labor supply findings of future UBI-related trials.

The most important things that experiments have revealed about the effect of UBI on time spent making money include the following:

• The labor supply response for all grant levels that have been tested (i.e., up to 150 percent of the US poverty line) is well within the sustainable range.

• A small grant, given to people who are deep in poverty (and not already working more than full time), tends to increase their hours worked and their productivity.

• A larger grant, given to people with incomes at or near the poverty line, will probably decrease their hours worked, but no evidence of mass withdrawal from the labor market has been observed in any study.

• Most people who have reduced their hours worked in response to UBI-related trials tend to fall into three categories: parents (usually mothers) spending more time caring for children; younger people spending more time in education; and recently unemployed people taking more time to look for the right job.

• Experiments conducted so far have not provided much evidence on whether replacing any particular program with an equal-sized UBI will increase or decrease their hours worked.[24]

• Most people who have reduced their hours worked in response to UBI-related trials tend to fall into three categories: parents (usually mothers) spending more time caring for children; younger people spending more time in education; and recently unemployed people taking more time to look for the right job.

As we interpret these and other findings about the labor market effects of UBI, it is important to understand the following points:

• No UBI trial, not even a saturation study, can measure the labor demand response to a decrease in labor supply associated with a national UBI. Trials will therefore tend to overestimate a UBI's impact on hours worked and underestimate its impact on wages, working conditions, poverty, and inequality. The amount of bias will vary greatly depending on the parameters of the experiment and the methodology of the simulation used to estimate national effects. There is no foolproof method to account for these biases.

• Targeting dramatically affects the results of any study and limits its applicability.

• Many reports simply present raw comparisons between control and experimental groups as if there were no targeting, no demand response, and no other effects that are unobservable in experiments.

• Most experiments conducted so far have been unable to differentiate what portion of the effects they observe is attributable to the size of the grant (the amount of money being redistributed) and what portion is attributable to the unconditionality of the grant (the fact that the money is redistributed in the form of a UBI rather than in the form of a traditional, conditional grant). The cost of removing this problem from experiments is high enough that we can expect this issue to affect most future trials, especially those conducted in wealthy countries.

• The absence of a decline in labor supply is only "good news" if you believe that low-income people are equitably paid and spending about as much time making money as they should right now. If you want UBI to help low-income people to command higher wages, better working conditions, and shorter workweeks, then you want a UBI sufficient to create a large (but sustainable) decrease in labor supply.[25]

Finally, UBI supporters should be aware that they can easily fall into a trap by using experimental evidence to disprove hyperbolic criticism of UBI (such as "no one will work" and "we can't afford it") by reporting the "good news" that the labor supply response was "small." This rationalistic response fails to appreciate that such statements are usually not meant literally. People who say something like "no one will work" usually mean something like, "I don't want any government spending going to any low-income person who reduces their labor time." For them, the labor supply response is never small enough.

Similarly, people who say "we can't afford it" don't usually mean that, objectively speaking, the spending required to support UBI is unsustainable; they mean that subjectively, it costs more than they think it is worth. If you don't like a policy to begin with, it's subjectively unaffordable at any cost.

No evidence refutes these subjective beliefs, and by trying to disprove figurative statements, UBI supporters often accept the premise that more labor from the middle and lower classes is everywhere and always a good thing. UBI is not the policy for people whose goal is to get low-income people to work as many hours as possible. The case for UBI is better built on the rejection rather than the accommodation of that belief.

ALASKA'S EXPERIENCE WITH UBI

Since 1982, the State of Alaska has paid the Permanent Fund Dividend (PFD), known popularly as the *Alaska Dividend*, to all of its residents.[1] The dividend is financed by returns to the Alaska Permanent Fund (APF): an investment portfolio created out of past state oil revenues.

The Alaska Dividend qualifies or nearly qualifies as a UBI under BIEN's definition. It is universal—paid to all permanent residents, even noncitizens. It is nearly unconditional, requiring only that people fill out forms to verify their residency. It is paid in the state currency. It is regular, in the sense that it's paid once a year, but irregular in the sense that the amount varies from year to year because the payments are determined by the returns on a fund created from past state oil revenues.

The dividend usually fluctuates between $1,000 and $2,000 per resident per year. It dropped to $1,114 in 2021 but rebounded to a record high of $3,284 in 2022. That figure amounts to $16,420 for a family of five.

The dividend has recently been attacked by Alaska's governor and legislature. In the face of declining oil revenues, some elected officials in those two branches of government have shown a preference for redirecting funds away from the PFD instead of reintroducing the state's income tax or increasing existing taxes.

Drawing on nearly forty years of positive results, consider six lessons to learn from the Alaska model.

Lesson One: Resource Dividends Work and They're Popular

The first and simplest lesson is that resource dividends work and are popular. Although the Alaska Dividend has recently come under attack from politicians, it continues to be extremely popular with Alaskans. It has helped Alaska maintain one of the lowest poverty rates in the United States. It has helped Alaska become the most economically equal of all fifty states.

Lesson Two: A State Does Not Have to Be Resource-Rich to Have a Resource Dividend

One might assume the Alaska Dividend is possible only because of Alaska's oil windfall. But consider three reasons that you do not have to be resource-rich to have a resource dividend.

First, Alaska isn't unusually rich. It ranks only tenth in GDP per person, and its GDP per person is only 14.5 percent larger than the average state.

Second, Alaska uses only a small fraction of its resource wealth to fund the APF. Its oil-industry taxes are low by international standards, and it doesn't tax its other resource-exporting industries as heavily as oil. Estimates show that the APF and PFD would be several times their current size if the state had aggressively devoted its potential resource revenues to it.[2]

Third, every country, state, and region has valuable resources. Estimates show that the "resource-poor" state of Vermont could support a dividend larger than Alaska's current dividend, if it made judicious use of resource taxes. Singapore is arguably one of the most "resource-poor" countries in the world because its population of millions is crowded together on a small island that imports almost every good its residents consume—but Singapore has fabulously valuable real estate. A tax on land value could be used to support a similar dividend.

The distinction between resource-rich and resource-poor communities should probably be discarded, because in most cases "resource-poor" communities are rich in the types of resources governments typically give away to wealthy corporations, while "resource-rich" communities are rich in resources governments usually charge for.[3]

Lesson Three: Look for Opportunities

Alaskans don't have the dividend because they are resource-rich; they have it because they took advantage of the opportunity to charge for a common resource when it was being privatized. Oil was discovered on state-owned land, and the state's then governor, Jay Hammond, was intent on making sure every Alaskan shared in its benefits. Common resources are being privatized all the time all over the planet, but governments usually give them away to corporations who sell them back to the public, profiting not just from any value the corporation adds, but also from the value of the resources it received for free.

It is much easier to impose taxation as a condition of privatization than it is to impose taxes later. Every new mine is an opportunity to assert community control of resources. So is every new smokestack or tailpipe that seeks to use the atmosphere as a garbage dump. Every business that needs a new bailout is an opportunity for the community to demand a share in the ownership of the business's assets.

Some opportunities are less obvious. For example, in 2005, the United States government gave away a huge portion of the broadcast spectrum to private companies for digital television broadcasting. If they had auctioned off leases to the highest bidder, they would have raised billions of dollars per year. If people and politicians stay on the lookout for opportunities to raise new revenues to support a UBI, they will find them.[4]

Lesson Four: Think beyond Profit Maximization

One possible danger of a resource-linked UBI is that citizens might want to sell more resources to make more money, perhaps doing even more damage to the environment. The solution to this problem is the realization that to assert the community's right to charge for the use of common assets is to assert the community's ownership of resources. Owners don't maximize profit by selling off resources as quickly as possible. They restrict sale to get the highest possible price.

We might have reason to restrict sale even more than necessary to maximize profit. A nation's resources are useful for more than sale. They are useful and valuable just as they are. We need to think of common resources as the nation's endowment. Our goal should be to maximize the long-term value of the whole endowment, not just in financial terms, but in terms of what they provide for the well-being of the people who live here now and who will live here in the future.

When we start to think of the commons as the people's endowment, we can raise prices above the profit-maximizing level. We can have more money coming in from the people who put the greatest demands on our resources while we also secure larger parks, more nature reserves, less pollution, better resource management, and stronger infrastructure.

Anyone who is worried that a dividend will buy off individuals' environmental diligence should remember that polluters have been degrading our environment for thousands of years without buying off the people. Nobody got a dividend when the Maori hunted the New Zealand moa to extinction. Nobody gets a dividend for the arsenic in our water or the sulfur dioxide in our air. Because the community has not asserted ownership of the commons, companies have been free to think of it as unowned and up for grabs. We have let them do with it as they please, taking valuables from—and dumping waste into—the environment we all depend on.

The right to compensation is part of the right of ownership, and along with ownership comes the right to manage, regulate, and restrict access. Receiving payment for resources helps community members think of themselves as joint owners of the environment with the power to demand tenants be good stewards of it.[5]

Lesson Five: Build a Constituency

As argued previously, universal programs that create feelings of shared benefit and shared ownership tend to build larger constituencies than targeted programs.

Receiving payment for resources helps community members think of themselves as joint owners of the environment with the power to demand tenants be good stewards of it.

Another way to build a constituency is to be significant. Small, gimmicky programs might be easier to pass, but they are also easier to cut when a less favorable administration comes to power. Significant programs tend to be more resistant to attack, and even then, opponents are usually only able to attack them piecemeal. The Alaska Dividend has only been able to be reduced, not eliminated entirely, because Alaskans have very good reason to care about it. The PFD makes a difference in their lives.[6]

Lesson Six: Avoid Creating an Opposition

The flipside of building a large constituency is to avoid creating an opposition. Policies such as the minimum wage and rent control put most of the burden on one specific, easily identifiable group that will fight the program as long as it exists. Even programs financed by a broad-based income tax can create an opposition if people connect the burden of paying taxes with programs they see themselves as unlikely to need.

Although some politicians covet the APF and would like to redirect its returns, the fund and dividend have no specific enemies: no one feels burdened by their existence because they don't cut into anyone's perceived ownership. Companies bid against each other for the right to pay into the fund to obtain drilling rights. It doesn't make sense for them to complain. The state owns the oil fields. Anyone who wants to drill must pay. That's just the way of the world.

But notice how atypical that model of the world is. Usually, the state awards ownership of resources to corporations for free. Anyone who wants to use those resources must pay corporations. And *that's* the way of the world.

We can change the way the world works.

Once the idea is firmly established that taxes and regulations reflect community ownership and custodianship of the environment, there is little for an opposition to build around. Companies will bid against each other for whatever access rights governments allow.

The APF and PFD came under serious attack only when the state's budget faced a crisis. The APF and PFD are on sound financial footing, but the rest of the state's budget isn't. No program is safe unless the entire budget is financially sound and politically functional.[7]

Conclusion

Alaska's fund and dividend are models we can build on. They were created largely because one person, Governor Jay Hammond, was in the right place at the right time. He was influenced in part by the second wave of the BIG movement, but his primary motivation was to ensure that every Alaskan tangibly benefited from Alaska's oil. He recognized that a UBI was the program most able to do that. Hammond had particularly favorable—but not unprecedented—circumstances. Future opportunities won't necessarily be as big and obvious as Alaska's oil windfall, but if we look, we will find them. And small opportunities add up if we take advantage of them.

We should also look back at already-privatized resources. Once we recognize that Alaskan oil companies should pay market rates for the oil they privatize, we could recognize that Hawaiian hotel companies should pay market rates for the beaches they have privatized. Perhaps every resource-extraction industry should pay for the resources it uses. Perhaps every polluter should pay for the damage they do to our environment. Perhaps all landowners should pay back for the resources they hold.

The cannabis industry would be willing to pay a sizable amount in exchange for national legalization. The producers of alcohol, tobacco, and any other drug we might choose to legalize could be made to pay for the strain they place on our healthcare system plus a tidy profit that we could use to support UBI.

Access to the broadcast spectrum does not have to be given away as it is now: it could be rented to the highest bidder. Bankers and investors could pay market rates for the risk the Federal Reserve Board socializes for them.

If we look for opportunities like these, we'll find more than enough of them to counteract the inflationary effects of a livable UBI.

THE CHOICE BETWEEN MANDATORY AND VOLUNTARY PARTICIPATION

Arguing for (and against) UBI

I hesitate to name a chapter "Arguing for UBI" because most chapters contain some argument about the desirability or feasibility of it. Chapter 1 began with an ethical argument. Chapter 2 showed that UBI can fill in many of the gaps in and eliminate a lot of the wasted expense of the traditional social policy system. It argued that a real UBI, which is genuinely both unconditional and universal, is more comprehensive and cost-effective than means-tested programs, including UBI's close cousin, NIT. And it demonstrated that UBI is affordable and sustainable and that there are plenty of tax and regulatory policies that can finance or resource it. Chapters 4 and 5 discussed the impressive array of empirical evidence about the effects of UBI.

Together these chapters have shown that although UBI might have far-reaching consequences, in and of itself, it is a mild reform. Income doesn't have to start at zero. If we can free ourselves from the commitment to mandatory participation, we can have a thriving market economy without poverty, homelessness, or the fear of economic destitution. Children would grow up better fed, safer, better educated, and better prepared to thrive as adults. Caregivers would be freer to pay full attention to the loved ones who need them without worrying how they both will survive. We would make it possible for people receiving benefits to enter the labor market without the fear that they would sacrifice eligibility if they lose or have to quit their job. We would reverse the growth of inequality through at least three channels: by direct grants, by giving workers greater power to command better wages and salaries, and by taxes on people with higher income and wealth.

What more do you need to know to conclude that we should introduce UBI? Some UBI supporters do stop their arguments here. The solution to one of our biggest economic problems—making sure everybody's needs are met—is not economically difficult.

But an argument that stops there fails to address the biggest sources of opposition to UBI: pro forma commitment to the property rights of the wealthy and/or to mandatory participation for everyone else. So I return to the line of ethical argument that began the book and consider the significance of the choice between voluntary and mandatory participation. UBI supporters who sidestep or downplay this issue can lose an audience to an opponent who plays the supposed responsibility of "everyone" to "work" like a trump card, overriding any interest in all the practical good UBI can do.

UBI will not sneak into policy without people noticing that it creates a voluntary-participation economy. The case for UBI needs to put the mandatory-participation economy on trial and show how weak the argument for it is.

The Essential Reason I Support UBI and a Voluntary-Participation Economy

It's wrong to come between anyone else and the resources they need to survive. But that's exactly what we do. Our rules deny the vast majority of people access to the resources necessary to produce food, shelter, clothing, and the other things humans need unless they continue providing services for existing property owners. Because our rules have that feature, we are all owed at least enough cash compensation to buy goods instead.

Humans are the only animals that have to ask permission to use the earth's resources. Wild animals don't have to ask permission to hunt or graze. Plants don't have to ask permission to photosynthesize. For most of the time humans have been on this planet, we didn't have to ask permission either. We could hunt, gather, fish, or farm on the earth's land. But over the last few hundred years, the resources of the earth have been divided into private property, and most of us didn't get a share. Instead, we got an unofficial but very effective obligation to work for those who got shares. And after only a few centuries living this way, we've mistaken it for our natural condition.

People often say that work is a fact of nature, but that's not true in the way we use *work* today. *Work* in the sense of "toil to convert resources into consumption" might be a fact of nature, but *work* in the contemporary sense of "time spent providing services for people who have money so you can get money to access resources" is no fact of nature. The current necessity of it is entirely the result of rules that have been imposed on us.

If you doubt that rules create poverty, consider why Americans can't build a house and farm as Henry David Thoreau did for a short time. Rules say they have to buy land first, and most of us can't afford it. Every time you see a physically able person who can't afford access to the resources they need to survive, there is some human-created rule making it so.

We can change the rules.

One erroneous defense of the mandatory-participation economy is to deny that it exists by pointing to the option of self-employment. Unfortunately, self-employment sounds much freer than it is. Self-employed people (who aren't already independently wealthy) have to work for clients, landlords, and banks, or their work is for nothing. Self-employed people might not take direct orders, but they serve the owners of external assets as much as anyone else. If they refuse, they'll eventually find themselves with no capital to work with, no shelter to sleep in, and no food to eat.

The correct term for someone who doesn't have to work for the people who control external assets is not *self-employed*: it's *independently wealthy*. That is, the only way you can be free from the need to provide services for the wealthy few is to be one of them—and most of us will never make enough to join that group.

People sometimes defend mandatory-participation by denying the role resources play in production and suggesting that virtually all inequality can be attributed to value created by owners. People can create at least some wealth for themselves without depriving anyone of resources. Say that you and I both start out with equal shares of resources. You improve yours. I deplete mine. We now have unequal wealth and unequal access to external assets without you having deprived me of anything.

That kind of story can and does happen, but it's a poor explanation of why most inequality exists in the world today and of why so many people are born and live their whole lives without independent access to enough resources to keep them alive. The land in our cities (where most of us need to live to participate in our economy and society) is expensive beyond the reach of all but the wealthy few. If we wanted to embody the ideal in which people who own wealth do not deprive others of resources, we would need some universal policy, like UBI, to ensure everyone does in fact have legal access to the resources they need to survive and thrive.

Another response is to deny that there is any element of force in the system because no single employer forces any single employee to work for them. The business owner simply offers employment to people who might want it. This is true at the individual level: I don't ask you to blame any particular owners. Instead, I ask you to think about the system. Rules effectively force members of the 99 percent to work for at least one member of the 1 percent of people who control access to the land and capital people need to work with to survive.

The ability to refuse any *one* employer is not true freedom. Freedom is independence: the power to say no to any and all masters, bosses, and superiors if one so chooses—to work only for oneself or to live off one's own assets. We might exercise independence by doing something other than paid labor; we might use it to bargain for better wages and working conditions within the paid-labor system; we might use it to learn better skills and reenter the market in a way that makes a bigger contribution and receives a bigger reward; or we might decide we're happy doing what we do right now. But whatever we do, it will be an unforced choice, not one made to avoid the threat of destitution.

I call this an *indepentarian* argument for UBI because it stresses respect for each individual's independence. It is *Paineist* in the sense that it relies on the observation Thomas Paine made about our property system back in 1797.[1]

The problem is not particular to private property or the market economy. If all resources were publicly owned and individuals could not access them without permission of public officials, that system would be just as much a mandatory-participation economy as capitalism is today. UBI is fully compatible with a private property system, as it is with many forms of social democracy and socialism.

If you think the market economy is going to fall apart without the forced participation of 99 percent of its workers, you must think it's a very fragile system. I've argued previously that there's every reason to believe a highly livable UBI is sustainable. Our system is not so fragile. We can afford to respect the independence of the least among us without fear that such respect will cause our economy to fall apart.

Labels such as "socialism" or "communism" are primarily used as meaningless scare words for any progressive policy. So many different ways to organize an economy are possible that it is folly to portray a continuum between "capitalism" and "socialism" as if it were all there is. There are thousands or millions of policy choices, all of which create differently working systems. UBI is actually rather individualistic, giving power to middle- and working-class people against both private and governmental power structures. It's compatible with any system that respects everyone's power to say no.

Incentives

UBI helps fix the biggest incentive problems in the market today: the lack of incentive for employers to pay living wages to their least-advantaged employees and to share the gains of economic growth with all of their employees. As discussed in chapter 4, this incentive problem is a central cause of poverty, inequality, and stagnant wages despite increasing productivity.

Of course, that's not what people usually mean when they say, "What about incentives?" They often mean that they fear "lazy workers" won't work if it is possible for them to remain alive and housed even if they don't take available jobs.

If "everyone has their price," then the laziest person in the world will work if jobs are attractive enough. If so, every time one person offers a job that another person doesn't want, the two parties are disputing wages and working conditions. Yet when the subject is whether workers want available jobs at going wages, you always hear about "lazy workers" who won't work (for going wages), but never about "cheap employers" who won't pay the wages you need to get people to work voluntarily. No matter how unattractive wages and working conditions might be, our society judges people to be bad if they don't take whatever jobs are available.

We don't moralize most economic transactions in this way. Nobody blames "lazy businesspeople" for pricing automobiles higher than the amount they're willing to pay. Outside the labor market, nobody seems to think of the inability to agree on a price as an ethical problem. If buyers and sellers can't agree to a price, the deal is wrong—not the people. We only regularly moralize when the buyer is an employer and the seller is a potential worker. We hardly notice that complaining about "lazy workers" involves taking the side of the more privileged party in a dispute.

Remember that UBI is a *basic* income. It is not the same income for everyone regardless of what they do. A good UBI is a base to live on, but higher incomes—often much higher incomes—are available in the market for people who perform work society recognizes as useful. UBI is structured so that people always end up with more (after all taxes and transfers) if they earn more privately.

In that context, the responsibility for work incentives belongs to employers. If one person has a task that they want someone else to do, they should pay enough that someone wants to do it. Offer wages and working conditions that are more attractive than living solely off UBI. That's how *free trade* works in a genuinely *free market*—where everyone is free *not* to trade, where both employers and employees have the power to say no to a bad deal.

In the economic sense, UBI has no work disincentive at all. What UBI gives people is the freedom to choose not to work rather than an incentive to avoid work if they find wages and working conditions attractive. Perhaps the fear is that UBI gives people *too much freedom* to choose whether to spend time making money or not. The following section addresses that issue.

The Work Ethic, the Moneymaking Ethic, and the Principle of Reciprocity

The term "work ethic" means different things in different contexts. Probably its most relevant definition is the principle that everyone who can must work for what they get. But if that's it, then the market economy is not now, nor has it ever been, consistent with any work ethic.

The essence of capitalism is return on capital. The passive, unearned rentier income capital provides is the system's goal and driving force. If you have a sufficient amount of capital, then you and your successors can live off a stream of income forever. Many families have lived off rentier income for centuries. The independently wealthy, as we call them, can work if they choose, and many of them do, but they have the option to live off the stream of income our rules provide for them. Management of one's own business is labor, but owners are not obliged to manage their own assets if they don't want to.

If the work ethic is a principle of justice, it must be applied to everyone or to no one.

Our society has no work ethic. It has, at best, a *money-making ethic*, as evidenced by the ability to buy yourself out of any genuine obligation to "work" with an inheritance, a lucky lottery ticket, lucky investments, or nefarious business deals.

UBI does not solve all the injustices associated with existing inequality, but it solves this one: the uneven application of the mandatory-participation requirement, in which most of us are held to an obligation to contribute labor to production, but the wealthy have no reciprocal obligation to work if they don't want to. Instead of trying to find some way to hold everyone to an equal obligation to participate in economic production, UBI equally relieves everyone from that obligation.

The work ethic argument is supposed to be motivated by a deeper principle of reciprocity, which basically means that what's good for the goose is good for the gander. Supposedly, if we apply this principle, everybody who gets something should give something back, and supposedly UBI or any unconditional policy violates it.

Our society has no work ethic. It has, at best, a *moneymaking ethic.*

The problem with this argument is that the existing distribution of property is inconsistent with reciprocity, just as it is inconsistent with the work ethic. Property rights exist because governments enforce rules. Although we are all animals who have evolved to depend on the earth's resources and environment, our rules say the earth belongs to some and not others. People who own the resources of the earth (and the external assets we make out of them) have a government license to interfere with everyone else who might want to use those resources, but not everyone gets a license, and the law enforces no *reciprocal* obligation for them to compensate people without such licenses.

People might have received their property by working for past owners, but work doesn't create property: rules do. The institution of property exists because governments make and enforce rules privatizing resources. All property on the earth (including electronic property) is made at least in part out of resources.

There are at least three ways to make access to resources consistent with reciprocity. First, we could share access to all resources equally without making it into property (as we do with the atmosphere and as many agrarian and foraging peoples have done with the land). Second, we could divide resources equally. Third, people who have more could pay compensation to people who have less. This last one involves UBI, and it is the only one of the three that is consistent with both reciprocity and a robust trading economy.

The UBI payment is *both* unconditional and reciprocal. Although you are not being paid for work you have done, you are being paid for rules that give other people an otherwise nonreciprocal advantage over you and that have been imposed on you without your consent. You can use your UBI not just to buy access to resources but also to buy services provided by others. The right to purchase those services is your compensation.

UBI, as I envision it, is a system in which those who control, use, or use up more of the earth's resources and the things we make out of them give something back to those who therefore must make do with less access to resources than they would if resources were commonly available or divided equally. If you receive more than you pay, that's your reward for making a smaller demand on resources than the average person. If you pay more than you receive, that's your fee for making a larger demand on resources than the average person. That's reciprocity.

The payment has to be unconditional to make up for the nonreciprocal allocation of rights to resources in the first place. If you have to work for a payment, that's a wage: wages are for labor; they can't double as compensation for lost access to resources.

Compensation is always unconditional. Somebody who breaks your leg has to compensate you in cash. They would be wrong to say, "I'll compensate you with a job. I can't just pay you for your broken leg unless you work for it.

That's something for nothing." A broken leg is something. A system of rules that gives some other group of people control over the resources we all depend on for survival is something too. UBI is not only consistent with reciprocity, it is a tool to preserve reciprocity.

The Circle of Obligation, the Safety Net, and the Social Contract

The last section argued that if we aren't going to apply the work ethic to everyone, we shouldn't apply it to anyone. A reasonable response would be to say that we really should apply the work ethic to everyone—rich and poor alike.

I don't understand how we could ensure that wealthy people actively work without either taking their wealth away or introducing a very different economic system.

In addition, the reciprocity problem is bigger than people who live solely off their wealth. The labor market is no meritocracy: many privileged people are held to a much lighter work obligation than less privileged people. They are allowed to fulfill it with variously high-paying, easy, stimulating, challenging, engaging, and/or enjoyable occupations, while less privileged people have no other reasonable choice but to take low-paying, difficult, disrespected, and unpleasant jobs. How easy, highly paid, or pointless can one person's job be and still count as fulfilling a genuinely *reciprocal* obligation to work with someone whose job is low paid, arduous, and essential? That's the kind of ethical question we'd have to wrestle with if we were to take seriously the idea of applying a work ethic to everyone. I don't think we're ready to seriously address that question.

We could introduce a national service in which everyone—rich and poor alike, no exceptions—at age eighteen worked for a year or a set number of years in equally demanding and equally necessary jobs, such as caring for the sick, disposing of garbage, or cleaning public buildings. We could then conceive of the UBI for ourselves and for our children as a type of pension for public service. If we, the privileged, don't want to force ourselves to do unattractive jobs even for a few years, perhaps we should not use the threat of economic destitution to effectively force less privileged people to do these jobs for a lifetime.

Ignoring these flaws, the ideal of the conditional safety net seems attractive. It is based on an imagined "social contract" with a circle of obligation in which everyone shares in the work and everyone shares in the benefits of the joint project we call our economy. Everyone promises to work if they can; in return they receive a fair wage if they can work and generous support if they can't. People who take this view believe that just about everyone in need can prove they're deserving in one of these two ways. Once we make them prove it, we'll feel solidarity for them and provide generous, secure support: free from stigma and invulnerable to political attack. Virtually everyone will see the benefit of meeting the real but doable conditions.

The conditional safety net has never fulfilled that promise even for people who meet its conditions. Conditional programs have not eliminated poverty—not among all people, not among all laborers, not among the people who meet virtually anyone's definition of being truly needy or deserving. Conditional programs haven't protected recipients from stigma. Adherence to conditions hasn't protected programs from political attack.

Conditions that mandate labor market participation for all who are able put the vast majority of individuals in the worst possible starting point in the market. They will be dismissed as "undeserving" if they object to wages and working conditions. That makes them vulnerable to low wages, poor working conditions, harassment on the job, and so on. Because we put workers in this vulnerable starting point, our policymakers are always trying but never succeeding to counteract vulnerability with labor market regulation.

Because potential workers have no reasonable alternative to participation, the imaginary agreement is more of a social ultimatum than a social contract, and that's part of the reason the conditional safety net has consistently failed to fulfill its promises. Social contract theory supposes that democratic decisions are *everyone's* decisions

—that everyone has agreed on some standard of fair reward for fair contribution.

In reality, even if everyone participates in the decision-making process, the best a democracy can do is obtain the decision of a majority. In any political system, the ruling coalition tends to be made of relatively advantaged people who don't always adequately appreciate the concerns of the least powerful, least advantaged group of people. We should not "privilege-splain" to the poor and oppressed by telling them how we've judged their situation to be good enough to mandate their participation.

Don't tell other people when you've ended their oppression. They'll tell you.

Psychological theory and historical experience indicate that ruling coalitions will suffer from self-serving bias like everyone else. Even in a perfect democracy, the ruling coalition might not have sufficient empathy for or understanding of outsiders and disadvantaged people to be capable of judging them. The farther you go from the centers of power, the more people's lives deviate from decision makers' expectations, the more their stories are untold, the more their situations are misunderstood, the less weight their concerns are given.

And our democracy is far from perfect. Our government is dominated by wealth and other forms of privilege, and the terms of our social ultimatum reflect the self-serving bias of the privileged group. The rest of us need the leverage UBI can give us to rebalance power.

Many specifics of the conditional system also reflect self-serving bias. For example, privileged people justify the participation requirement by arguing that jobs give people a sense of purpose. That's a paternalistic rationalization and a poor reason to force people to take what often turn out to be dead-end jobs. Showing respect for disadvantaged people would entail freeing them to decide whether a job provides enough sense of purpose—along with pay and other rewards—to be worth taking.

The self-serving assumptions built into our system are in many ways self-defeating for most of us, in part because political authorities promote the values they display rather than the values they demand from others. The mandatory-participation requirement is supposed to promote unselfishness. People in need of help are supposed to learn the virtue of giving back when they receive, but the principle the authority promotes by example is selfishness: never give unless you get something back.

People in need in a mandatory-participation economy will rightly question whether the authority has their best interest at heart when the authority's first question is, "What can you do for us?" And they will be reasonable to react by thinking, "When I was in need, they gave me nothing without demanding something in return. I will never give them anything unless I get something in return." Our political authority promotes selfishness because it behaves selfishly. If you want to promote unselfishness, you must give unselfishly.

Probably the most important way in which the self-serving assumptions of the mandatory-participation economy are ultimately self-defeating is that they're really only good for employers who like to pay low wages. Mandatory participation is bad for employers who like to pay high wages because mandatory participation puts downward pressure on wages, making it harder for high-wage employers to compete.

In the same way, mandatory participation is bad for dedicated, hardworking laborers. As the "Incentives" section argued, you don't help workers by putting them in the position in which they can't refuse to work. By taking away leverage from virtually all workers, our increasingly punitive mandatory-participation policies have led to greater inequality, lower salaries and wages, greater workplace insecurity, greater stress, and so on, not just for people at the very bottom but for almost everyone with a job.

One might respond that the reality behind the circle of obligation is that sooner or later people really do need each other. That is true, but that doesn't mean anyone needs to force people to do things for each other. If we want people to do things, we can use other tools—such as good pay, good working conditions, genuine respect, and greater access to resources—to get people to do the things we want done.

As good as it might sound to create a circle of obligation where everybody pitches in and everybody shares the reward, it has a cruel aspect. A system with conditions can never eliminate poverty: if the conditions for getting out of poverty are real, some people won't meet them. If the conditions are so easy that everyone can meet them, they're not really conditions at all.

The conditional approach to poverty needs some poverty to exist forever to maintain adherence to its conditions. As much as we like to think otherwise, that's cruel. The threat of poverty and homelessness hangs over the head of everyone who doesn't believe they've been offered a fair reward for a fair contribution and everyone who falls through the cracks of our highly imperfect system.

UBI would be a new kind of check on our political process, conceding real, practical power to every single individual as an individual, not just as a member of a constituency. No matter how disadvantaged, no matter how far from the center of power, they have the power to say, "No, you have misjudged what a fair contribution and fair wage is. You let privileged people reap high rewards for easy work of questionable value, and you expect me to do the worst jobs at the lowest wages for the least respect. I will not work for you until you give me wages and working conditions that I find acceptable."

A voluntary-participation society can't ensure that everyone will work, but it can ensure that everyone can afford food, shelter, clothing, and the other material necessities. It can reduce the fear and stress of middle- and lower-class lives. It's a kinder society. It invites you to do the things society recognizes as useful by offering you rewards, but it doesn't force you to do what you're told by hogging all the resources if you refuse.

Good for Workers

A similar response to UBI puts the complaint in terms of exploitation. Although giving potential workers the power to opt out might redress an issue between potential workers and rentiers, it might cause a problem between those who actually opt out and those who remain at work. Most of the goods UBI beneficiaries will buy require labor; their demand for goods will create inflationary pressure that will have to be counteracted by taxes levied in part on workers. Therefore, one might suppose that it allows nonworkers to exploit workers.

The exploitation objection presumes a recognizable dichotomy between "workers" and "UBI recipients." In fact, even if we think of work only as "time spent making money," the vast majority of UBI's net beneficiaries are current workers, retired workers, underage children of workers, caregiving dependents of workers, and so on.

Chapter 2 showed that a modest UBI system is a direct net benefit to nearly 50 percent of households and that a more generous plan extends direct benefits to 70 percent of households. The vast majority of people in that group are paid workers and their dependents. Although UBI is not conditional on work, this structure ensures that many or most workers receive a direct financial benefit from it.

The number of workers who benefit from UBI increases again as one considers for what portion of a person's life they must work to qualify as a "worker." Most people who live entirely off UBI *at any given time* will have worked significant portions of their lives. They might choose to take time off for training, for education, to care for children or relatives in need, to escape harassment or violence from an employer or spouse, to find a better job, to start over in a new region, to attempt to start a business, or just to enjoy life temporarily.

As a university professor who has taken several sabbaticals, I know from experience that it would be a good thing if all workers were free to take a sabbatical like me. Sadly, under current rules, many of the least advantaged Americans who do the most difficult, thankless, yet—as we learned during COVID—essential work will never have more than a few weeks off during the years they are capable of working.

The number of workers who benefit from UBI increases still more if one questions the dubious assumption that work should be understood as time spent making money. Some non-moneymaking activities contribute much more to society than some moneymaking activities. Compare, on the one hand, care work, volunteer work, and being a friend to someone who needs one to, on the other hand, marketing addictive substances as long-term painkillers, trying to get elderly people to sign up for dubious investments, and trying to get children hooked on food that will make them unhealthy.

The fraction of workers who do not receive a direct financial benefit from UBI at any point in their lives is likely to be rather small and very privileged. It would be made up of people who have never lived in low-income families (even as children); people who never wanted to take a few months off work or who were wealthy enough to self-finance their own sabbatical; people who had enough private income to sustain them while raising children or going through training, education, or unemployment.

That observation indicates that workers who are net financial contributors over their entire lives are probably the most privileged, highest-income workers. It is doubtful many people who could get such attractive jobs would turn them down to live on a $12,000 or $20,000 UBI. My job is one of the attractive ones. I'm a professor with a low teaching load, a good salary, and a lot of time to do self-directed research and writing. I wouldn't turn my job down to live on a UBI of $12,000 or $20,000, but if the essential worker who cleans the toilets in my office did, it would be rather unseemly for me to accuse them of somehow exploiting me. And if some people in that position opt out, it's very possible the people who continue to clean toilets would get better wages and working conditions.

These observations bring me to another problem with the belief that UBI financially harms or exploits workers: The worst thing you can do to workers is to put them in the position in which they have to work to survive. The power of workers to walk away both individually and on mass is their power to command good wages and working conditions. You can call it leverage or market power, but simple supply and demand works similarly.

The more people there are who compete for jobs like yours and the more they desperately need those jobs, the more they bid down wages in your sector of the labor market. Imagine that all the people who are currently out of the labor force suddenly became ready, willing, and able to do your job. That might be good for overall production, but it won't necessarily be good for you and the other people working in your sector now. It will certainly be good for employers in your sector because they can pick the workers who can work the longest hours for the lowest pay in the worst conditions.

The worst thing you can do to workers it to put them in the position in which they have to work to survive.

Good for Women

All of the arguments presented so far apply to women at least as much as they do to men. Women make up about half of the workforce, and women are disproportionately subject to harassment, low wages, poor working conditions, and disrespect on the job. UBI is good for *pink-collar workers* (people in traditionally female-dominated professions) both because it gives them the power to refuse bad jobs and because it acts as a direct subsidy to people who remain in low-wage jobs.

One criticism of UBI is that it could reinforce traditional gender roles. When people get greater ability to provide full-time, unpaid care for children, the disabled, or the elderly, women will be more likely to do it, and as they do, they will reenforce the social expectation that these tasks are women's work.

But many women are performing these tasks now without a UBI, and often without any government support at all. They and the people they care for are paying a terrible price for it. Single mothers and their children are the poorest group in the United States, and their position has gotten worse in recent decades, a trend often called the *feminization of poverty*. If we want to help women, we need to stop punishing people who do care work. By providing unconditional aid even to people who are doing something more important than making money, UBI would instantly reverse the trend toward the feminization of poverty.

On the issue of traditional gender roles, it is not certain that the overall effect of UBI would be to reenforce them. It's true that UBI makes it easier for women to do unpaid care work, but it also makes it easier for men to do the same. UBI will make it more affordable for men and women to share care work if they choose, and men and women might use the power UBI gives them in the workplace to demand the flexibility they need to hold a job and do care work at the same time.

The power to say no, the importance of which I've stressed throughout this book, needs to be understood in a broad sense. It's not just about men saying no to bad jobs. It's about the empowerment of all vulnerable people in nearly all social interaction. Women and girls are often victimized because they are financially vulnerable. There are women who live with abusive men or tolerate sexual harassment on the job because they will be hungry or homeless if they refuse. If an above-poverty-level UBI is introduced, there will be fewer incidents of violence against women, spousal abuse, sexual harassment and rape on the job, sexual exploitation of children, and other forms of gendered domination and violence. UBI will not eliminate any of these problems, but the power it gives to women will help reduce all of them.

Good for People of Color

Significant structural disadvantages for people of color exist in the United States. These disadvantages will not go away until US citizens work together to eliminate them. UBI will not eliminate structural disadvantage, but it can help.

Most people of color are workers, and half of people of color are women, and so all of the arguments from the "Good for Workers" and "Good for Women" sections apply to people of color as much as they apply to anyone else. In fact, those arguments might apply to people of color more than to white people because people of color are more likely to be in low-end jobs, more likely to be vulnerable in their personal and professional interactions, more likely to live in high-poverty areas, and less likely to have wealth or family wealth to fall back on during times of acute need.

UBI is not reparations for slavery or for other forms of racial and ethnic injustice, but it is money, and the net benefit of this monetary transfer will go disproportionately to people of color because, on average, people of color have disproportionately low income and wealth. Therefore, it will begin to do many of the things that reparations are supposed to do, such as helping to reduce the racial wealth gap, reduce the education gap, reduce the number of people of color stuck in dead-end jobs, reduce power differentials, and so on.

One of the main barriers to the introduction of UBI in the United States is probably white prejudice. The attitudes we have in our heads about "lazy workers" might be, in part, a vestige of hundreds of years of the racialized belief that *some people* just don't want to work. White decision makers aren't counting themselves or their close supporters among "some people." White Americans (myself included) need to come to terms with the racialized history of such images. The mere introduction of UBI will require the nation as a whole to show a little more respect for people of color.

I said at the start of this chapter that people will not introduce UBI without noticing that it creates a voluntary-participation economy. In addition, no one will fail to notice that people of color are included in the group who are relieved from the burden of mandatory participation. We have to embrace this as a good thing, as a sign of respect. The country that forced Black people to come here as chattel slaves and made it impossible for Native Americans to continue to survive by their own efforts should now scrupulously refuse to force disadvantaged people of any ethnic group to work for more advantaged people.

Better Than Alternative Reforms

One could concede that the UBI plans under discussion would be an enormous benefit to many if not most workers relative to the existing conditional system, but still hope for some other plan that would leave out the true non-contributors, save the money it gives to them, and benefit workers even more than they benefit under the UBI plans I've discussed. This section discusses such alternatives purely from the perspective of the benefit to workers to show that work-requirement-friendly programs are very often not worker-friendly programs.

Two commonly discussed alternatives of this kind are participation income (PI) and a federal job guarantee (FJG), both defined in chapter 1. PI provides an income for everyone judged to be *participating*, which includes not only paid labor but also many nonmarket activities, such as care work and approved volunteer activities. It is designed to be a mandatory-participation-friendly alternative to UBI, using the broadest conception of "work."[2]

An FJG provides a job for anyone who wants one without regard for whether they are willing or able to work in the private sector. It is not necessarily an alternative to UBI. It has other functions and could be introduced alongside UBI. But I address it here only as a potential mandatory-participation-friendly substitute for UBI.[3]

Both PI and an FJG can do good things. They both ensure a minimum level of income for workers, and an FJG, by competing with private-sector employers, sets a minimum standard for wages, hours, and working conditions.

A generous PI or FJG could increase living standards at the low end of the wage spectrum.

But I doubt that either of these programs will do as much for workers as a good UBI can. Many of the benefits of UBI for workers are not available (or not as readily available) from an FJG and PI. These include the ability that UBI gives workers to take a sabbatical, to take time off to start a business, relocate, educate oneself, negotiate for shorter work hours, and so on.

Many of the disadvantages of these programs, from the workers' perspective, exist because unlike UBI, an FJG and PI submit less-privileged workers to judgment by more-privileged people. Someone has to decide if they're performing well on their "guaranteed" job or doing a sufficient amount of the right kinds of nonmarket activities to qualify as "participating" and, therefore, as worthy of having enough money to afford food, shelter, clothing, and the other necessities of life. If their contribution is judged insufficient, they have to submit to a second round of judgment to determine whether they are eligible for some other program (e.g., disability) targeted at people who haven't proven themselves in the PI or FJG program.

Judgment is imperfect. Undoubtedly, some people who really are participating will be judged unworthy, and others who really aren't will be judged worthy.

Judgment is unpleasant and stressful for the person being judged, and it creates feelings of antagonism, especially when the stakes are so high. UBI does not create a world without judgment, but it does create a world in which no one needs to fear being judged unworthy of having an income sufficient to afford adequate food, shelter, and clothing.

Judgment is costly. Both PI and an FJG involve an enormous overhead cost that UBI does not. Imagine the expense of determining whether every person who says they're volunteering actually is. The PI needs inspectors all across the country to determine who's doing what volunteer work and whether they are doing it well enough to qualify. These will need to be well-paid professionals who could be doing other, more valuable work. Judgment is especially costly to the neediest recipients. As a privileged worker, I will receive my PI extremely easily. I'll just have my accountant share my tax forms with the PI system. A less-privileged woman who lives in a low-income area and who is providing care work for her ill sister and her sister's three children is unlikely to have an accountant and will probably have difficulty finding the time, filling out the forms, and providing whatever verification the PI or FJG authorities require to prove that she is participating in the way she says. Even if she can eventually prove it, she will have wasted a great deal of her extremely valuable time and effort.

An FJG program needs an office in every city and every little town all across the country. The buildings have to be stocked with the right tools for FJG workers to use on their jobs. These buildings will need bosses, administrative assistants, accountants, compliance officers, and so on. Not all of these jobs can be done by FJG workers. The FJG agency will have to bid people away from the private sector to take these management jobs. All of these overhead expenses count. All of them reduce the resources available to benefit workers.

On the other side of the cost equation, even if judgment were costless, these judgmental programs don't save very much money because they don't exclude many people who would qualify under UBI. An FJG and PI would create all the judgment expenses mentioned previously in order to eliminate paying a UBI to the relatively small amount of people who would be judged unworthy. There is not enough money to be saved by eliminating payments to the small portion of people who never work and aren't eligible for disability or other need-based programs to make it possible that an equal net amount spent on PI or an FJG would provide more benefit for workers than UBI.

Judgement doesn't make people's needs go away. After we judge that people are unworthy of an income large enough to meet their basic needs, those people continue to exist. They will continue to have needs and to try to fulfill them. Many of them will become homeless, and so will their children. Many will beg. Many will visit food pantries and soup kitchens. They will visit emergency rooms much more often than better-off people. These things are extremely costly in terms of money and resources, and that cost leaves less available to benefit workers, which is supposed to be the goal of mandatory participation.

Judgement empowers judges in ways that aren't always good for the people being judged. This problem makes PI particularly vulnerable to what I call *employer capture*. That is, some of the benefits intended for workers end up going to the companies that employ them. Because workers have to keep their jobs to keep their PI, it's as if the program pays part of their wages for them. That gives employers the incentive to try to get some of the benefit of the government's effective subsidy for themselves, perhaps by reducing wages or allowing work conditions to deteriorate.

Benefits could also be captured by charities or non-profit organizations whose "volunteers" suddenly become a dependent workforce. One could imagine universities, churches, and other nonprofits replacing paid janitors, food-service workers, and other low-end jobs with "volunteers" who are treated as employees with wages in the form of PI. Some of the people empowered to decide whether a particular "volunteer" is working hard enough to qualify for PI will probably abuse that power.

A PI program would have to introduce measures to counteract all these forms of employer capture. These measures would cost resources, and they would be imperfect.

They would increase the expense of the program without eliminating employer capture.

UBI is not completely invulnerable to employer capture, but it has one countermeasure built in: if employers are capturing some of the benefit of UBI, workers can quit and live off their UBI. They don't need to find some approved alternative form of participation to maintain a livable income. They can do the one thing PI and F walk away.

An FJG is largely invulnerable to employer capture because it competes with rather than subsidizes private-sector wages. As mentioned earlier, an FJG gives workers leverage against private-sector employers who have to match or improve on the working conditions set for FJG laborer. This argument is true, as long as private-sector firms and nonprofits are prohibited from subcontracting FJG workers. If such subcontracts were allowed, FJG would become highly vulnerable to employer capture.

In addition, the leverage FJG gives workers is only as good as the FJG jobs themselves. FJG gives workers no leverage at all against the FJG system itself. And this makes an FJG particularly vulnerable to what I call *administrative capture*—that is, the problem in which some benefits are diverted from the intended recipients to the people in charge of running the program.

Will every FJG boss in every little town be a good boss? Or will they abuse the power they have over workers for whom this job is their last resort before homelessness?

A woman who is sexually harassed on an FJG job she needs to keep her from homelessness is just as much a worker as the white male factory employees we picture in our heads when we hear the term "worker," but her work matters. If she is harassed, she is not better off with an FJG than with UBI. An FJG program will have to introduce measures to try to keep local bosses from abusing their power. These measures will cost resources, and they will be imperfect. The resources devoted to combating local mistreatment of FJG workers could be used to benefit workers in general, via a higher UBI or a lower marginal tax rate.

Administrative capture can happen at the national level as well. The people who propose an FJG are liberals who think of it as a program for the benefit of workers, and they conceive of good jobs with health insurance, paid sick leave, and other benefits in workplaces where employees are respected and cared for.

Observations of similar programs, such as workfare programs, Work for the Dole, and work experience programs, suggest that it doesn't always work out that way. FJG workers may be looked down on and treated paternalistically, as if the mere fact that they don't have a better job implies that there is something wrong with them. Jobs might end up being very low paid and without benefits. Federal, state, and local governments might lay off well-paid union employees and replace them with low-paid FJG workers, who have no leverage against whatever wages, hours, and working conditions are set by privileged decision makers in Washington. If the FJG program fails to produce good wages and working conditions in FJG jobs, it will fail to improve private-sector wages and working conditions.

It is by no means certain that FJG jobs will turn out this way, but the program is politically vulnerable to these problems in a way that UBI is not. UBI is largely invulnerable to administrative capture because administrators have no power over UBI beneficiaries. Their job is simply to distribute checks as Social Security administrators do. After nearly ninety years, Social Security remains one of the best-administered government programs with the lowest overhead cost. We could expand on that model by creating Social Security for All in the form of UBI.

One of the most important reasons UBI will be better for workers than PI or an FJG is that it gives them leverage against all employers—private and public. Repeating my earlier point, the worst thing you can do to workers is put them in the position in which they have to work to survive. PI and an FJG fail to give workers what they need most: the power to say no to any and all employers who might take advantage of their otherwise vulnerable position.

The only way you can harm UBI beneficiaries is to set the UBI too low, but unlike abuses that could happen when the level of a PI or FJG is too low, a too-low UBI doesn't give anyone power over UBI beneficiaries. The vast majority, which includes the middle class, will have reason to resist decreases in the UBI because they receive it too. And the solution for a too-low UBI is clear: raise the UBI and index it to the cost of living.

UBI won't be enough to make up for all injustice against disadvantaged people, but at least it gives them the power to refuse to contribute to a system if they believe it takes advantage of them. We cannot eliminate all injustice, but we can respect people enough to say, if you find the work options available to you to be exploitive, you don't have to accept them. I can't imagine a better tool to fight exploitation and improve life for workers.

If you want to help workers, concede power over their lives to them and respect their choices.

The "Natural" Right to Private Property

Most of the arguments against UBI addressed thus far are based on our mutual obligations. This final section addresses an argument based on our *lack* of mutual obligations. One could say people have a right to their property. They worked for it or got it in some other form of voluntary transfer, such as a gift. Therefore, we should accept whatever distribution comes out of the free operation of the market economy, no matter how unequal it might be. On this basis, one might argue that any taxation, regulation, and redistribution of property for the benefit of less-advantaged people violates a natural right to private property, and that, as an involuntary transfer, it makes people less free from interference.

This argument is not specific to UBI; it suggests that any form of redistribution involves an infringement of natural rights (and perhaps all or most taxation and regulation do so as well). A person who accepts this argument, might conclude that, those less fortunate should appeal to voluntary, private charity rather than to the government.

In response, UBI is not a bad deal for wealthy people. All people, including the wealthy, get a safer, cleaner, healthier, kinder, less-stressful nation. We get rid of areas filled with people living in tents. We reduce all the associated costs of poverty and extreme inequality. Employers get a better educated, happier, and more able work force. Employers pay higher wages, but it's worth it, and our nation is not so cheap that we need to pay poverty wages anyway. All you have to do is pay your taxes, obey regulations, and respect people who might exercise their power to say no to your job offer.

Charity has a poor record of addressing poverty. Many charities support paternalistic programs that try to fix or convert the underprivileged. A lot of charitable giving actually perpetuates rather than reduces inequality (e.g., by giving to universities attended overwhelmingly by the children of the elite).

I've argued that UBI is fully compatible with a robust market system in which most resources are privately owned, but property owners do need to pay their taxes and obey government regulations to ensure that resources are available to make UBI viable.

Whatever good UBI might do, some property rights extremists argue that freedom trumps anything a government might do by interfering with the rights of property owners. Even people who favor redistribution often concede that there is a naturally unequal right of private property that supposedly supports freedom and equality before the law but in fact conflicts with equality of any other kind—even if they are willing to override those concerns to achieve other goals.

This section argues that the claims of property rights extremists should not be conceded. Capitalism, as currently constituted or as envisioned by its more radical defenders, does not deliver freedom from interference and equal rights under the law. Although the problems I discuss are fundamental, we don't necessarily have to overthrow the whole system to fix them. My argument here is only for sufficient taxation and regulation to support UBI.

Natural rights–based arguments for the existing distribution of property tend to focus on the actions of individuals within the system rather than on the system itself. If property rights in external assets exist, and we trade them, then whatever distribution of property comes out—no matter how unequal—is (in part) the result of voluntary actions of people, who had the legal right to decide whether or not to take those actions.

This explanation distracts from the interference and force that exist in the background. Before people can trade external assets, the resources that assets are made out of have to be privatized. Governments have used an enormous amount of force and violence to create and maintain the private property system. That force is aggressive interference that reduces the freedom of people who get little or no share of property in external assets.

When asked about this issue, private property extremists usually discuss a principle of "appropriation" and tell a fanciful story about the imaginary "original appropriator": the first person who chose to go into a virgin wilderness, cut down the trees, plant crops, and thereby establish the first private property. From that starting point, we can imagine trade, gifts, and other voluntary exchanges, getting us to the highly unequal world we live in today.

We can imagine it, but is that what actually happened? When asked this question, people who portray property as a natural right usually admit that the story is fiction. It is not meant to show what actually happened but what *could have* happened.

Why is this one story about what could have happened relevant? Is it the only thing that could have happened? Why is it any more relevant than any other story one might tell about what could have happened? Is it more likely than other stories?

Property rights extremists tend not to address these questions head on, but they tend to portray this story as what *would have* happened if people had been free to exercise their natural rights without interference throughout history. If the story of original appropriation has any value at all, it must illustrate what people actually try to do when free from interference.

If an examination of history showed that people continually attempted to appropriate land on an individual basis and use it to create a private property system and that other systems were created by latecomers wanting to interfere with private appropriators, then it would indicate that there is something to the concept of a natural right to private property. Unfortunately, most people who take this view produce no evidence to support it. Those who cite any evidence at all tend to cite the same few cherry-picked examples that tell them what they want to hear.[4]

Grant S. McCall (an anthropologist at the Center for Human-Environmental Research and Tulane University) and I made an extensive review of the relevant evidence in our book, *The Prehistory of Private Property*. It shows that the earliest people to use or work with resources—whenever free from interference—almost everywhere in the world tended to establish complex, flexible, overlapping, and at least partially common rights to land and resources so that every member of the community had access to the resources necessary to meet their needs, but not necessarily to any particular plot of land. Such arrangements have existed in foraging communities in the arctic, the tropics, and temperate zones in all continents, and in small-scale agricultural communities all over the world, including in medieval and early modern Europe. Such property systems lasted in some parts of Europe until as late as the early twentieth century.

The form of private ownership now often portrayed as "natural" is a late development. Everywhere that we have records of its establishment, the institution was forced on people by aggressive governments—most especially through the enclosure movement in Europe and the colonial movement elsewhere. In virtually all known cases, people strongly resisted being pushed off the land to make way for elite ownership.

This evidence strongly contradicts the belief that private property rights without responsibility for redistribution are in any way natural. That institution was established by governments in acts that constituted aggressive interference with common people who had been using land and natural resources for centuries. Governments did it for the benefit of elites. And they have never held elites responsible for compensating common people for their lost access to land and resources.

Therefore, the highly unequal right of private property that exists today is not a natural right but a legal construct that can be changed and must be modified if we're going to make our system consistent with equality before the law.

Even if a highly unequal property system doesn't follow from the free exercise of any natural right, one might suppose that it promotes freedom by allowing the unfettered exchange of goods once established. This claim might be a good reason not to throw out all private property rights, but it gives no reason to reject the responsibility of people who own more resources and the external assets we make out of them to compensate those who own less. We can enjoy the benefits of trade and still pay our taxes, and we have to if we want all people to be free to decide whether or not to trade.

As argued earlier, without redistribution, a private property system effectively establishes mandatory participation for the vast majority of people, who simply must work for bosses, banks, clients, and landlords to remain alive.

Yet private property extremists feign indifference to participation. The rights-based argument for private property is supposedly about the relationship between owners and their property rather than about the relationship between owners and nonowners. Property rights do free owners from interference by giving them power to use resources in any way they want, but those same rights also give owners the legal right to interfere with anyone else who might want to use the resources their property is made out of. That interference is the very fact that creates the mandatory-participation economy. The reason most inhabitants of the world have to give at least some of their labor to bosses, clients, banks, and landlords is that we need their permission to legally access enough resources to keep us alive. The natural property rights argument is not about promoting freedom for everyone but about selectively declaring that some interference doesn't count—especially the interference that creates a mandatory-participation requirement for nonowners.

Writings from the colonial and enclosure movements show that both the people who established the private property system and the people who were dispossessed by it were well aware of the power it would give owners (as a group) over nonowners. It's a prime reason elites wanted to establish the system and why common people resisted it.[5] The same ideas are echoed by people who say that UBI will reduce the incentive to work—meaning to accept jobs at the going wage, under current working conditions.

If we want to promote freedom as noninterference *for everyone*, the people who get to control the earth's resources need to make a reciprocal payment to the people who don't, as I suggested earlier and as I argue more extensively in several books.[6] Without a reciprocal compensation payment, unequal private property is inconsistent with both the goal of promoting freedom from interference for all and the principle of equality before the law.

Property rights advocates argue that the value of resources is negligible. What's important, they say, is the value that people have added to it. This argument has three problems. First, and most importantly, the question is not how much resources are worth to people who buy and sell them, but what costs they impose on nonowners. This cost is not measured by the market. Because no one asks nonowners how much it is worth to them to lack access to resources, the market puts no price on it. There are many costs to being a nonowner, one of the most important of which is the loss of independence caused by being effectively forced to work for at least one member of the group of people who own a sufficient amount of external assets. How much is independence worth to everyone who has had it taken away against their will? The answer, of course, is that independence is priceless. This is why we don't allow people to sell themselves into slavery or indentured servitude. If we realize that the choice of which boss, bank, client, or landlord to work for is not genuine freedom, I believe we will see that a UBI at least large enough to meet a person's basic needs is essential to preserving freedom in a property-based economy.[7]

Second, if it were true that resources aren't valuable, people wouldn't fight so hard to keep the world's resources in the hands of the privileged. We wouldn't be chopping down the last of our rainforests to get land for our production system. We wouldn't think twice about giving away forty acres and a mule right on Manhattan Island for anyone who preferred it to the jobs on offer. The facts are very much the opposite: even the remotest places in the United States are unavailable to people who don't want to participate in our economic system.

Third, the value added by people wasn't all added by owners. Owners' claims to land and other resources trace back to government grants and colonial aggression. Private owners hire workers to improve the value of land, but unless those workers are independently wealthy, they have no legal means to survive other than to work for property owners. It's hard to give owners much credit in a system in which most of the value is added by people who had no other choice than to provide services for property owners.

Another way to defend property rights without any responsibility of redistribution is to argue that observations like these are unimportant because an unfettered private property system makes us all so much better off that quibbling about how to divide those benefits is unnecessary. This argument quietly drops the connection between unequal property rights and freedom. It's actually a paternalistic effort to justify interference with common people supposedly for their own benefit. It also happens to be false.

Grant S. McCall and I debunk this claim in one of our books. We use extensive empirical evidence from anthropology and history to show that although the average person might be better off, the least among us are worse off than they could reasonably expect to be in a stateless society with common property rights. As difficult as life was for prehistoric or stateless people, the life of many homeless people is worse.[8]

A society where the threat of homelessness hangs over the heads of a mass of people is a cruel society with a one-sided conception of freedom. We don't have to live with these aspects of our society. We can get rid of them by introducing a UBI large enough to meet people's basic needs.

AUTOMATION AND UBI

One argument for UBI seems to have the potential to make the mandatory-participation debate moot. According to this argument, automation will soon replace so many jobs that we never again have to worry about making a contribution to production by labor. The vast majority of work—and virtually all of the drudgery—will be done for us by machines. Humans can concentrate on other things that make life interesting and meaningful, and UBI will become inevitable.

This argument tends to divide audiences down the middle: some people immediately believe this day is right around the corner; others instantly conclude it's crazy to believe it'll ever happen. My view is in-between. The popular prediction isn't crazy, but it's not necessarily right around the corner either. I believe, an alternative automation-based argument–based on the past and the present rather than on a prediction of a possible future—is more important to the case for UBI. This chapter explains both the popular automation-based argument for UBI and the alternative argument.

The Popular Automation Argument for UBI

The usual story connecting automation and UBI is not about how automation is affecting labor right now but about the fear that so many occupations will soon be automated that massive unemployment will result. When this happens, many technology experts and IT industry leaders believe, the demand for labor and employment will drop precipitously. There simply will be no demand for all the labor people are capable of doing. We'll be faced with two choices: allow most of the world's labor force to become beggars, or create something very much like UBI so that people can live and thrive in a world with very little paid labor. The choice is so stark, they say, UBI will become inevitable.

This argument has become increasingly popular since the Great Recession, and it has accounted for a significant portion of the increase in support for UBI over that period. But consider five reasons to fear that it also turns off a lot of other people and gives new ammunition to UBI opponents.

It Strikes Many People as Unrealistic

In the past, going back hundreds or thousands of years, automation has always eventually led to more employment rather than less. For example, in the late 1700s, more than 90 percent of American laborers worked on farms. Today, less than 1 percent do. That means, more than 90 percent of the previously available jobs in the United States have already been automated away, but many more jobs and arguably better jobs have replaced them. If we hadn't automated agriculture, we wouldn't have had the labor we needed to produce all the railroads, cars, trucks, planes, computers, and other new things we have today.

This observation is not proof. Just because automation has always meant more jobs in the past, we cannot conclude it will always mean more jobs in the future. Empirical evidence shows that factors of production can and do become obsolete, and when it happens, it tends to happen quickly. Horses were outmoded in almost all industries in a matter of decades after thousands of years of steady work. We can't rule out the possibility that human labor—or some large segment of the labor force—could become outmoded in a similar time frame.

The argument is not unrealistic, but for the purpose of the political debate, it may be enough that it sounds unrealistic to many people.

Even If It's Possible, It Might Not Happen Any Time Soon
Even if we could prove that automation will eventually eliminate the need for most human labor, that doesn't prove it's going to happen any time soon. According to the St. Louis Federal Reserve Board, the employment-to-population ratio has not varied much in the last seventy years. It's fluctuated between about 55 percent and 65 percent. The rate in September 2021 (58.7 percent) was down about six percentage points from its high in the late 1990s, but it was higher than at any time in the 1950s or 1960s.

An argument for UBI based on the predicted collapse of labor demand can't rely on the claim that that collapse *might* happen or even that it *will* happen someday. It must convince people that the collapse *is happening* so quickly that now is the time to act. It might be impossible to make that argument before people actually witness the prediction come true.

The Risk of Discrediting the Argument
Overly strong predictions about future automation might discredit the argument if the pace is slower than predicted. The concern that automation could replace most human labor is not new. The most influential economist of the twentieth century, John Maynard Keynes, talked about greatly diminished need for human labor in the near future as early as the 1920s. Concern for future automation was a major driver of the guaranteed income movement

in the 1960s, when the employment-population ratio was lower than it is now.

Even if tech industry leaders are generally right, the changes they foresee might take longer than they think and are likely to affect some segments of the market long before others. Surviving sectors might absorb enough labor to keep demand rising for decades. If so, the automation-inspired UBI interest of the 2020s might soon look as dated as Keynes's predictions of the 1920s. We cannot know for sure.

Automation Might Not Look like Automation

When people hear about robots replacing humans, they usually imagine an ever-increasing unemployment rate. Although there has been some decline in employment since the Great Recession of 2009, there is no big trend in this direction so far.

The economy is structured so that the vast majority of people need jobs to survive, and therefore they'll take whatever they can get if they have to. People who have been displaced by automation (or by anything else) will flood whatever occupations are most likely to take them—usually low-wage and contingent-labor ones.

If so, automation might be more likely to cause increased inequality and precariousness than to cause the widely predicted increase in unemployment. Although the expected trend toward ever-increasing unemployment has not been seen, the trend toward increasing inequality *has* been going on for the last fifty years or so. If displaced workers drive down wages in already low-wage sectors, there is no telling how long the automation of labor will manifest as increased inequality rather than increased unemployment.

The Argument Gives Ammunition to UBI Opposition

If your argument is, "We need UBI because someday automation will eliminate almost all demand for labor," then it is logical for people to reply, "Let's wait to see when that day comes." I've discussed many reasons throughout this book for why UBI is long overdue. An argument based entirely on the belief that we *will* need UBI at some point tacitly (and, wrongly, I believe) concedes that we don't need UBI now, when in fact generations of people have been suffering in ways UBI can relieve.

One might respond by saying that automation is happening so fast that these issues don't matter. If it's not apparent now, it will be in five years. We should look at this prediction in historical context. People have been making the argument about the coming urgent need for UBI based on the advance of AI, robotics, and self-driving cars since the great recession a dozen years ago. Chapter 2 mentioned that Robert Theobald and Buckminster Fuller thought the sudden loss of jobs was imminent during the computer revolution of the 1960s. The eminent economist John Maynard Keynes argued in the 1920s that the loss of jobs would happen before the end of the twentieth century.

An argument based entirely on the belief that an enormous change is right around the corner risks discrediting itself if the change doesn't happen as fast as claimed. People will begin to respond, "OK, when outlandish prediction finally comes true, we'll talk about your reform. Until then, we'll forget all about your idea."

If I'm right that UBI is overdue, the argument for it has to be based on the here and now. But as the next section argues, automation does have a part to play in that argument.

An Alternative Automation Argument for UBI

The following present-based arguments connecting automation and UBI are at least as compelling and more pressing than the argument based on future levels of employment.

The Side Effects of Automation Have Been Disrupting People's Lives for Hundreds of Years

Whether automation eventually increases or decreases employment, it disrupts the labor market and people's lives every year. The industrial revolution might evoke images of farmers' children happily leaving the countryside for good jobs in the city, but automation doesn't always—or even usually—happen that way.

People are not interchangeable parts. Automation takes people who have acquired skills that command good wages and says, "We don't need you anymore. Go to the bottom of the unskilled labor market." When this happens, it drives down wages and working conditions for many sectors in the low- and middle-income labor market. Even sectors with rising demand can see declining wages if they're drawing people from an increasingly precarious national labor force.

Many displaced people never recover. Even the lucky ones who eventually work their way back to a job as good as the one they lost often go through a period of trauma. Sometimes they lose their homes or have to declare bankruptcy. Their children suffer along with them. Even a temporary period of poverty can scar children for life.

Technological unemployment is not new. In the early 1800s, the Luddite movement sprang up among English textile workers, who found their well-paid, highly skilled jobs were being replaced by textile mills that employed low-paid workers and required them to work long hours in poor conditions. The term *Luddite* has come to refer to any person with an opposition to technological improvement, but the real Luddites weren't necessarily opposed to automation itself; they were demonstrating against the cruel way our labor market reacts to automation. When the skills they'd been encouraged to learn were made worthless, they were given nothing to cushion the loss of income. They had no other choice but to spend the rest of their lives at the bottom of a very unequal labor market in which they had to work long hours in harsh conditions for low pay. The possibility that their children or grandchildren might eventually get better jobs would have been little comfort.

We do not know whether the current round of technological change is the one that will finally cause the long-predicted permanent decline in the demand for labor, but we do that the pace of technological change is displacing labor at an increasing rate, disrupting more people's lives than it typically has in the past. The present pace of automation demands a UBI now.

We don't need to stop technology to fix the problems that inspired the Luddites. We need to raise the floor to ease the transition. The solution is not to keep the economy from changing. No one has the right to keep an increasingly unneeded job forever. Just because you're a skilled coal miner, truck driver, autoworker, or university professor doesn't mean that the rest of the world has to keep paying you to do that job for the rest of your life whether they need that contribution or not. Whether technological advancement increases, decreases, or has no effect on the overall employment level, it will displace some workers and business owners. One humane solution is UBI, which cushions the blow while giving people the ability to take the time to learn new skills without stressing about survival, so that they may contribute in some new and different way.

Most of Us Haven't Shared in the Benefits Automation Has Created over the Last Fifty Years

One central reason we all need UBI is that most of us haven't shared in the benefits that automation and economic growth have made possible over the last half century. Between the 1920s and the mid-1970s, wages and the median income tended to rise with national income. But since then, almost all the benefits of economic growth have gone to the top 1 percent of the population.

As mentioned earlier, the per-person productive capacity of the United States roughly *doubled* between 1980 and 2020. That means we could all consume twice as much without working any more than we did in 1980, work half as much without consuming any less, or consume more and work less in any combination in between. But very few of us are allowed to. Families making the median income have gained far less than GDP has increased. Wage workers have gained very little. Minimum wage workers make less in real terms now than they did in 1955—sixty-six years ago—when our economy had less than one-third the productive capacity it has now.

Imagine if our incomes had kept pace with economic growth: A minimum wage worker could afford to pay rent

One central reason we all need UBI is that most of us haven't shared in the benefits that automation and economic growth have made possible over the last half century.

and raise children. The median wage worker could work twenty hours a week and live decently. Instead, virtually all the gains we've all helped produce have gone to the wealthiest 1 percent, very few of whom are technological innovators. Most of the 1 percent simply own resources and the things we've made out of them in the past.

People like to say that's just the market. But it's not *individual actions* in the market that have caused this enormous increase in inequality. It's *the rules we make* for the market. Wages kept pace with growth in the mid-twentieth century because we had a progressive tax system, more generous social services, and a less-powerful donor class. Since then, we've changed the tax system so that the rich pay a smaller percentage of their income than the lowest-wage workers, and the government has given out more corporate welfare to already highly advantaged people. With these changes, wealthy people have bought more and more real estate (in areas where zoning laws and other regulations greatly limit new construction), driving up the cost of housing for everyone, and in turn giving the rest of us a greater need to work long hours.

At the same time, we've changed the rules in ways that consistently reduce workers' leverage. We've made it harder for employees to organize unions and for unions to bargain for higher wages. We've gutted the welfare system through a combination of eliminating programs, reducing benefits, and making conditions more punitive. As workers lose their leverage in the market, employers lose incentive to share the benefits of automation with them.

In this environment of growing inequality, increased technological displacement exacerbates the problem, further diminishing worker leverage and increasing inequality. And so, we find ourselves in the position in which our economy has doubled in size and most of us have not shared in the gains.

To reverse this situation, we need new rules that are more favorable to the 99 percent. UBI does more than cushion the blow to displaced workers. It improves all workers' power to demand a larger share of the benefits of automation that we and our ancestors all helped to create.

Conclusion

I've offered two automation-based arguments for UBI. Neither of them is about future predictions. In fact, these arguments imply UBI is long overdue—perhaps hundreds of years overdue. We need UBI to protect the 99 percent from disruptions caused by automation. We need UBI to counteract the imbalance of power that automation has helped create between the people as a whole and the small group of people who own the resources we all need to produce things. And we need UBI to help just about everybody get a share of the benefits of automation.

THE FUTURE OF UBI

The future is inherently unpredictable. But I find several reasons to believe that UBI will remain a focus of academic research and that the political movement for UBI will continue to grow.

Research from Here

The academic debate over UBI is thriving and likely to continue across the disciplines of social science and philosophy.

Right now, UBI-related experiments are the most rapidly growing area of UBI research. As I write, more than one hundred small-scale experiments are going on across the United States. Some of them are targeted—for example, looking at the effect of UBI on trans people, on young adults leaving foster care, and so on. Others are more generalized. A few larger-scale experiments are being conducted around the United States and around the world. GiveDirectly's large-scale, long-term experiment will go on in Kenya for quite some time, and GiveDirectly continues to raise money to conduct new experiments. Other experiments are being organized around the world. As the results of these experiments trickle in, they will renew interest in empirical research on UBI in the fields of sociology, economics, public policy, and so on. But experiments are only one part of the academic debate over UBI.

UBI is perhaps the most well-researched alternative to traditional social policy, making it an important part of both ethical and scientific discussions of public policy. Existing policies or proposals often get evaluated against the alternatives of UBI or of the absence of any policy to address the problem in question.

Normative researchers are increasingly dealing with issues such as mandatory participation and the power to say no. Although most researchers don't put these ideas in those terms, the framing of the debate seems to be changing. Political philosophers once widely accepted the claim that UBI beneficiaries would violate a value of reciprocity if they failed to accept employment. They now more often grapple with the argument that the existing distribution of property violates that very same value by imposing mandatory participation for less privileged people and no such requirement for the most privileged, while it is the relatively more privileged who decide what wages, hours, and working conditions the less privileged must accept. As the framing of the normative debate moves in this direction, the need for UBI becomes more apparent, and the weakness of the case for mandatory participation becomes more obvious.

The Movement from Here

The outlook for eventual adoption of UBI is encouraging. The financial crisis of 2009, the Great Recession, the COVID pandemic, and linked economic distress returned the attention of people around the world to issues like poverty, inequality, unemployment, and precariousness. The economic and political uncertainties since then have only increased that attention. People are looking for new solutions and different approaches, and there are reasons to believe that interest will continue to grow.

More than a century of experience with the traditional, conditional welfare model have revealed its weaknesses. It is no coincidence that middle-class income has stagnated over the same period that the welfare system has been slowly eroded away. The need for fundamental change in how we distribute access to resources and the external assets we make out of them has grown more apparent.

There are several paths to make it happen. Politicians like US President Franklin Roosevelt, British Prime Minister Clement Atlee, and Alaska Governor Jay Hammond have pushed through major progressive initiatives with the power of their office.

But the most reliable path to more progressive policy is more democracy. The most progressive governments in the world (such as the Nordic countries) are also the countries in which the people as a whole have the greatest power over government decision-making.

One perennial antidemocratic problem in American politics is the power of the donor class. Studies in the United States consistently show that legislation is far more responsive to the opinions of the wealthy than to the opinions of voters as a whole. Even politicians who want to do good for the people have to put enough goodies for lobbyists in the legislation to get them to back it. The way opinion has been going, it is very likely that a movement toward greater democracy in the United States will go hand in hand with a movement toward UBI.

Yet disturbing trends against the power of the people are present in the United States. Some state governments are attempting to establish permanent minority rule by disenfranchising voters, gerrymandering, and other antidemocratic tactics.

Perhaps the biggest threat to the UBI movement is the rise of right-wing nationalism. Although right-wing nationalists are always against progressive change, they aren't always as successful as they have been recently around the world. If and when nationalists succeed in convincing the mass of people that our economic problems are caused by some boogeyman instead of economic policy, they can halt progressive policy change. The boogeymen might be immigrants; foreigners; LGBTQ people; racial, ethnic, or religious minorities; and any other vulnerable group they single out. America is particularly vulnerable to right-wing nationalism because white fear and distrust has extremely deep roots.

But although right-wing nationalists can halt progress for a time, their success is almost always temporary because they don't deliver for the people. All they offer is conflict, and conflict does not solve the underlying problems that bring attention to them to begin with.

UBI might not always gain steam as fast as it has in the last few years, but UBI supporters have good reason to feel encouraged that the long-term trend of increasing support for UBI will continue even if more ups and downs are coming. Each wave of UBI support has been larger than the last. With every resurgence, UBI has been represented by more developed proposals, and supporters have been better prepared to address people's concerns.

The shortcomings of the existing system will not disappear. I have argued that they are inherent to the conditional model, and they will continue to provide a strong

Perhaps the biggest threat to the UBI movement is the rise of right-wing nationalism.

reason for people to look seriously at UBI. The millions of people actively demonstrating for greater equality today are not looking to rebuild Lyndon Johnson's welfare state. They're looking for a new approach.

One simple, effective approach needs to be tried: UBI, the approach that eliminates fear as the driver of our economic system. We need a policy that stops judging the disadvantaged and starts helping.

ACKNOWLEDGMENTS

Acknowledgments are difficult for me because I take a very long time to write anything, I send manuscripts to many people, and I present bits and pieces at many conferences. People give me lots of useful feedback, and invariably, over the course of the years, I often forget who said what when. Sometimes I think it's better to leave everyone out than to forget people who might have contributed as much as the people I remembered, but I'll try anyway.

My wife Elizabeth Smith Widerquist (known professionally as Elizabeth Rousselle) helps me in many ways, even if we seldom ask each other to read our research.

Chapter 5 summarizes work coauthored by Michael Howard. Thanks, Mike.

Chance Lacina read three drafts of this manuscript and gave me feedback as I developed it. Several other people gave me feedback on early drafts. They include Benedikt Zoepf, Chaonan Lin, Marvin Reusch, and probably some others. Two of my Georgetown research assistants, Anjali Singh and Muhammad Carter, proofread the last draft before I sent the book to the copyeditor. Alex Howlett gave me feedback on a section that I've since deleted from this book. Among his advice was to consider deleting that section. So, although he hasn't technically commented on anything in this book, he gave me good advice and contributed to the book's final form. Emily Taber, formerly of the MIT Press, gave me excellent feedback of her own and arranged for several anonymous referees who also gave me very good and very useful (if time-consuming) feedback.

I know I presented parts of this book at several conferences and received useful feedback, but I can't remember who said what, when, or where. The automation chapter, for example, began as a speech that I gave at several different venues, the most memorable of which being a talk organized by the New Orleans Yang Gang in early 2020. If you gave me feedback on this book in any context, and I've forgotten to mention you by name, thank you just the same, and know that your help was appreciated.

—*Karl Widerquist, at a street cafe called the Bean Gallery in the Souq Waqif, Doha, Qatar, February 2023*

Administrative capture
A public policy problem in which some benefits are diverted from the intended recipients to the people in charge of running the program.

Alaska Dividend
See **Permanent Fund Dividend (PFD)**.

Alaska Permanent Fund (APF)
A portfolio of investments held by the State of Alaska, used primarily to fund the PFD.

Arab Spring
A prodemocracy protest movement that swept the Arab world beginning in late 2009.

Automation
Technological improvements in production of goods and services; specifically, improvements that involve replacing human labor with machines or algorithms.

Basic Income
A term usually used as a synonym for UBI.

Beneficiary/net beneficiary
A person or family who receives more in UBI (or any other social program) than they pay in taxes.

Break-even point
Definition 1, for UBI: The point at which the taxes a person or a family pays equals the UBI(s) they receive so that they are neither net beneficiaries nor net recipients.

Definition 2, for NIT: The point at which benefits are fully phased out as income rises.

Capital
External assets used in the production process.

Categorical
An adjective describing traditional, nonuniversal programs, targeted at people who meet particular criteria of need or deservingness.

Child grant
A targeted basic income for children (see also **Refundable child tax credit**).

Citizen's income
A term usually used as a synonym for UBI.

Citizens pension
A government retirement program that is designed like a Basic Income for people over a certain age. Everyone above age X receives $Y regardless of private income, wealth, current work status, past work history, or any other factor except citizenship and/or residency.

Colonial movement
A term usually referring specifically to European imperialism outside of Europe, during which European governments tended to force conquered peoples to adopt European institutions such as private property rights in land and natural resources.

Commons (common resources)
Resources (especially land, air, and water) available for use by every member of a community but not the individual property of anyone.

Conditional cash transfers (CCTs)
Streamlined transfer programs that deliver regular cash to families that meet relatively simple eligibility criteria.

Conditionality
The requirement that recipients of benefits fit into some category, fulfill some requirement, or both to maintain eligibility.

Contributor/net contributor
A person or family who pays more in taxes than they receive in UBI (or any other social program).

Control group
The group that does not receive the treatment in an experiment. In a UBI trial, the control group receives no UBI but usually remains eligible for any other existing programs.

Cryptocurrency
Privately issued, digital forms of money.

Earned Income Tax Credit (EITC)
A refundable tax credit in the US that subsidizes low-income workers.

Employer capture
The public policy problem in which some of the benefits intended for workers end up going to the companies that employ them.

Employer of last resort (ELR)
See **Federal job guarantee (FJG)**.

Entitlement
A government program that provides assistance to individuals.

Enclosure movement
The gradual process of privatization of land in Europe when peasants were forcibly dispossessed of their traditional rights of access to land so that lords could legally establish private ownership.

Experimental group
The group receiving the treatment in an experiment. In a UBI trial, the experimental group receives a UBI.

External assets
All assets external to the human body, including natural resources and all the things we make out of them other than people.

Federal job guarantee (FJG)
A policy proposal in which the government would offer a job at the going wage to anyone who wants one.

Fiscal
An adjective for things pertaining to government tax and spending policies.

Fiscal space
The amount of unused economic capacity in a nation at a given time; if and when it exists, it creates the opportunity for increased government spending without the need for increased taxes or borrowing to maintain stable prices.

Flat tax
An income tax with one uniform rate for all levels of income with no tax deductions.

Food insecurity
A euphemism for hunger or malnutrition caused by lack of financial means (whether continuous or intermittent).

Food stamps
The popular name for the Supplemental Nutrition Assistance Program (SNAP), a federal program that gives food vouchers to low-income people.

Full UBI
Definition 1: A UBI high enough to live on.

Definition 2: A UBI high enough to replace all other redistributive programs.

These two definitions are not the same thing, and both are controversial. There is no agreement about exactly what level of UBI is enough to live on and whether any amount is enough to replace all other redistributive programs.

GiveDirectly
A private nonprofit company that runs a large UBI project in Kenya

Grant level
The minimum level of individual income ensured to everyone under any BIG plan.

Great Recession
A period of high unemployment that began with the financial crisis of 2008–2009 and lasted through the first half of the following decade.

Gross cost of UBI

The grant level of UBI times the number of recipients ignoring the amount of UBI that people pay themselves through taxes. Although this term has *cost* in the name, it is not a useful measure of UBI's cost in terms of UBI's opportunity cost or its effect on incentives or individuals' budgets.

Gross domestic product (GDP)

A measure of the level of economic activity in a nation.

Guaranteed income

Definition 1: Any unconditional program designed to ensure everyone has a nonzero income, whether means-tested (NIT) or non-means-tested (UBI). Also called guaranteed annual income, guaranteed adequate income, income guarantee, or basic income guarantee.

Definition 2: A unconditional program designed to ensure everyone has a nonzero income by any means other than through UBI.

Hold harmless

A provision in law ensuring that the replacement of one government program by another causes no financial harm to recipients of the original program.

In-kind benefits

Social policies that provide goods rather than cash—for example, public housing, public education, Medicare, Medicaid, and SNAP.

Livable UBI

One term for a UBI high enough to meet people's basic needs.

Luddite movement

An early nineteenth-century movement involving protests against and sabotage of textile manufacturers who were mechanizing production in ways that undermined the wages of textile workers.

Marginal tax rate

The amount income is taxed and/or benefits are reduced per dollar of income. For example, someone who has to give up $500 per week in unemployment insurance to take a job paying $500 per week in wages effectively has a marginal tax rate of 100 percent. If they also pay taxes on that income, their marginal tax rate is greater than 100 percent.

Means-tested benefits
Social welfare policies that are conditional on income, wealth, or people's assessed ability to obtain income and wealth.

Minimum wage
The legal minimum an employer is allowed to pay an employee. Some forms of labor (e.g., farm labor) are not protected by the US minimum wage law.

Modern monetary theory (MMT)
A nonmainstream economic theory that (among other things) stresses the truism that taxes don't actually "finance" spending. It is closely associated with FJG as a tool to maintain full employment and price stability.

Negative Income Tax (NIT)
A means-tested form of BIG, ensuring a nonzero minimum income for everyone but phasing out payments as the beneficiary's private income increases.

Net cost of UBI
The gross cost of UBI minus the amount people pay themselves by paying taxes. This measure of UBI's cost is useful for determining its opportunity cost and its effects on individual budgets and incentives.

Net redistributive effect of UBI
The amount UBI transfers from net contributors to net beneficiaries.

Opportunity cost
The amount of one thing someone has to give up to get another thing.

Partial UBI
Definition 1: A UBI too small to live on.

Definition 2: A UBI too small to replace all other redistributive programs. Both definitions are controversial (see **Full UBI**).

Participation income (PI)
A conditional basic income that requires some form of recognized participation, such as paid work, volunteer work, care work, disability, involuntary unemployment, and so on.

Periodic
An adjective to describe programs with regular payments over a long time span or over a lifetime rather than one-time or short-term grants.

Permanent Fund Dividend (PFD)
A policy that has paid a dividend to Alaskan residents since 1982. Although the dividend is small and although it varies from year to year, it qualifies as a form of UBI under most definitions.

Poverty
The lack of financial means necessary to secure a minimally adequate standard of living, or the lack of legal access to the resources necessary to meet one's basic needs.

Poverty line
The minimum income a person or family needs to escape poverty.

Poverty trap
An adverse incentive *not* to take a job or make more money so as to maintain eligibility for a social welfare program.

Privatization
The legal process of transforming a natural resource or a common asset into private property.

Property
Anything that can be owned, including external assets and a person's body and abilities.

Refundable child tax credit
A refundable tax credit targeted to children (see **Child grant**).

Refundable tax credit
An amount of money that taxpayers can subtract directly from taxes owed to their government and that (unlike a tax deduction) will be paid to them in cash if the tax credit is larger than the tax they owe.

Saturation study
A type of social science experiment or pilot project in which all people in a geographical area are tested instead of a random selection of people within the area in question.

Social dividend
A synonym for UBI.

Social Security for All
A proposal to integrate UBI into the existing Social Security system.

Social welfare policy/social welfare program
Any policy designed to reduce inequality or poverty, as well as any policy to secure and maintain individual well-being.

Stakeholder grant
A one-time unconditional payment usually given in a large sum when a person comes of age.

Supervisory
A characteristic of many traditional welfare programs in which recipients have to follow direction from an official or a bureaucracy to maintain eligibility.

Supplemental Nutrition Assistance Program (SNAP)
A federal program, popularly known as *food stamps*, that gives food vouchers to low-income people.

Targeted basic income
A nonstandard term for a basic income targeted at specific groups, such as basic income for artists, the disabled, the elderly, children, and so on.

Temporary Assistance for Needy Families (TANF)
A US federal program of block grants to state governments that allows states, within limits, to run their own welfare programs.

Unconditional
An adjective describing social policies that are free from requirements for recipients to perform a task or demonstrate need. This word is usually used to emphasize freedom from performance requirements.

Universal

An adjective describing social policies that are paid to every member of a political community (e.g., a nation or a region) or every resident of a geographic area without any requirement to demonstrate need or perform a service. It is usually used to emphasize the receipt by each member of the community regardless of income or other means they might have.

Universal Basic Income (UBI)/Unconditional Basic Income

A periodic cash payment unconditionally delivered to all on an individual basis, without means-testing or a work requirement.

NOTES

Chapter 1
1. Russell, *Proposed Roads to Freedom*.
2. According to the Basic Income Earth Network (basicincome.org).
3. Atkinson, "Case for a Participation Income."
4. Kelton, *Deficit Myth*; Tcherneva, *Case for a Job Guarantee*.

Chapter 2
1. Friedman and Friedman, *Free to Choose*.
2. This chapter draws heavily on Widerquist, "Cost of Basic Income."
3. Clark, "Economics of Poverty."
4. Widerquist, "Cost of Basic Income."
5. Again, here's a mathematical proof that net tax rates, average tax rates, and total tax burdens for all individuals are the same under NIT or UBI. See Andrew Saxe and Liz Fouksman, "The BIG Cost Confusion," https://efouksman.weebly.com/uploads/5/6/6/1/56610801/saxe_fouksman_2019_marginal_tax_talk.pdf. For further discussion of the gross- and net-cost issue, see Arndt and Widerquist, "Deceptively Simple."
6. Widerquist, "Cost of Basic Income."
7. Widerquist and Arndt, "Cost of Basic Income in the United Kingdom."
8. See Tom Neubig and Agustin Redonda, "Tax Expenditures—The $1.5 Trillion Elephant in the (Budget) Room," Bloomberg Tax, September 7, 2021, https://news.bloombergtax.com/daily-tax-report/tax-expenditures-the-1-5-trillion-elephant-in-the-budget-room.
9. Piketty, *Capital in the Twenty-First Century*.

Chapter 3
1. This chapter draws heavily on Widerquist, "Three Waves of Basic Income Support."
2. Widerquist. "Three Waves of Basic Income Support."
3. Milner, *Higher Production by a Bonus on National Output*.
4. Widerquist.
5. Widerquist.
6. Widerquist.
7. Greene, *The National Tax Rebate*.

8. Widerquist.

9. Widerquist.

Chapter 4

1. For more evidence, see Widerquist, Noguera, Vanderborght, and De Wispelaere, *Basic Income*; Torry, *Palgrave International Handbook of Basic Income*; Miller, *Essentials of Basic Income*; and sources cited throughout this chapter.

2. Wilkinson and Pickett, *Spirit Level*.

3. Wilkinson and Pickett.

4. Hanlon, Barrientos, and Hulme, *Just Give Money to the Poor*.

5. Hanlon, Barrientos, and Hulme.

6. Korpi and Palme, "Paradox of Redistribution and Strategies of Equality."

7. Torry, *Palgrave International Handbook of Basic Income*.

8. Torry.

9. Torry.

10. Widerquist, *Critical Analysis of Basic Income Experiments*.

11. Widerquist.

12. Levine et al., "Retrospective on the Negative Income Tax Experiments."

13. Forget, "Town with No Poverty."

14. Calnitsky, "More Normal than Welfare."

15. Haarmann et al., *Making the Difference*.

16. Standing, "Unconditional Basic Income."

17. Laín, "Basic Income Experiments."

18. Widerquist, *Critical Analysis of Basic Income Experiments*.

19. This section draws on Forget, "Town with No Poverty"; Calnitsky, Latner, and Forget, "Life after Work"; Calnitsky, "'More Normal than Welfare'"; and Laín, "Basic Income Experiments."

20. This section draws on Widerquist, "Failure to Communicate"; Widerquist, *Critical Analysis of Basic Income Experiments*; Gilbert et al., "Would a Basic Income Guarantee Reduce the Motivation to Work?"; Forget, "Town with No Poverty;" Calnitsky, Latner, and Forget, "Life after Work"; Calnitsky, "'More Normal than Welfare'"; and Lain, "Basic Income Experiments."

21. Widerquist, *Critical Analysis of Basic Income Experiments*.

22. Widerquist, "Failure to Communicate."

23. Widerquist.

24. Widerquist, *Critical Analysis of Basic Income Experiments*.

25. Widerquist.

Chapter 5

1. This chapter draws heavily on Karl Widerquist and Michael Howard, "Lessons from the Alaska Model."
2. Widerquist, "Exporting the Alaska Model to Alaska."
3. Widerquist and Howard, "Lessons from the Alaska Model."
4. Widerquist and Howard.
5. Widerquist and Howard.
6. Widerquist and Howard.
7. Widerquist and Howard.

Chapter 6

1. Paine, *Agrarian Justice*.
2. Atkinson, "Case for a Participation Income."
3. Kelton, *Deficit Myth*.
4. For a review of such arguments, see Widerquist and McCall, *Prehistory of Private Property*, especially pp. 127–146 and 178–193.
5. Widerquist and McCall, *Prehistory of Private Property*.
6. Widerquist, *Independence, Propertylessness, and Basic Income*; Widerquist, *Problem of Property*; Widerquist and McCall, *Prehistoric Myths in Modern Political Theory*.
7. Widerquist, *Independence, Propertylessness, and Basic Income*.
8. Widerquist and McCall, *Prehistoric Myths in Modern Political Theory*.

BIBLIOGRAPHY

Arndt, Georg, and Karl Widerquist. "Deceptively Simple: The Uselessness of Gross Cost in the Cost-Benefit Analysis of Universal Basic Income." *Maine Policy Review*, November 2019.

Atkinson, Anthony. "The Case for a Participation Income." *Political Quarterly* 67 (1996): 67–70.

Calnitsky, David. "'More Normal than Welfare': The Mincome Experiment, Stigma, and Community Experience." *Canadian Review of Sociology* 53, no. 1 (2016): 26–71.

Calnitsky, David, Jonathan Latner, and Evelyn L. Forget. "Life after Work: The Impact of Basic Income on Nonemployment Activities." *Social Science History* (2019): 1–21.

Clark, Charles M. A. "The Economics of Poverty in the United States of America." *Oikonomia: The Journal of Ethics and Social Sciences* 4, no. 3 (2005): 6–19.

Forget, Evelyn L. "The Town with No Poverty: The Health Effects of a Canadian Guaranteed Annual Income Field Experiment." *Canadian Public Policy* 37, no. 3 (2011): 283–305.

Friedman, Milton, and Rose Friedman. *Free to Choose: A Personal Statement.* New York: Harcourt Brace Jovanovich, 1980.

Gilbert, Richard, Nora A. Murphy, Allison Stepka, Mark Barrett, and Dianne Worku. "Would a Basic Income Guarantee Reduce the Motivation to Work? An Analysis of Labor Responses in 16 Trial Programs." *Basic Income Studies* 13, no. 2 (November 2018): 1–12.

Greene, Leonard M. *The National Tax Rebate: A New America with Less Government.* Washington, DC: Regnery Publishing, 1997.

Haarmann, Claudia, Dirk Haarmann, Herbert Jauch, Hilma Shindondola-Mote, Nicoli Nattrass, Ingrid van Niekerk, and Michael Samson. *Making the Difference: The BIG in Namibia: Basic Income Grant Pilot Project Assessment Report.* Windhoek: Basic Income Grant Coalition, 2009.

Hanlon, Joseph, Armando Barrientos, and David Hulme. *Just Give Money to the Poor: The Development Revolution from the Global South*. Boulder: Kumarian Press, 2010.

Kelton, Stephanie. *The Deficit Myth: Modern Monetary Theory and How to Build a Better Economy*. London: John Murray Publishing House, 2020.

Korpi, Walter, and Joakim Palme. "The Paradox of Redistribution and Strategies of Equality: Welfare State Institutions, Inequality, and Poverty in the Western Countries." *American Sociological Review* 63, no. 5 (1998): 661–687.

Laín, Bru. "Basic Income Experiments: Limits, Constraints and Opportunities." *Ethical Perspectives* 28, no. 1 (2021): 89–101.

Levine, Robert, Harold Watts, Robinson Hollister, Walter Williams, Alice O'Connor, and Karl Widerquist. "A Retrospective on the Negative Income Tax Experiments: Looking Back at the Most Innovative Field Studies in Social Policy." In *The Ethics and Economics of the Basic Income Guarantee*, edited by Karl Widerquist, Michael A. Lewis, and Steven Pressman, 95–106. Aldershot: Ashgate, 2005.

Miller, Annie. 2020. *Essentials of Basic Income*. Edinburgh: Luath Press Limited, 2020.

Milner, Dennis. *Higher Production by a Bonus on National Output: A Proposal for a Minimum Income for All Varying with National Productivity*. London: George Allen & Unwin, 1920.

Paine, Thomas. *Agrarian Justice*. Benjamin Franklin Bache, 1797.

Piketty, Thomas. *Capital in the Twenty-First Century*. Cambridge, MA: Harvard University Press, 2014.

Russell, Bertrand. *Proposed Roads to Freedom*. New York: Blue Ribbon Books, 1918.

Standing, Guy. "Basic Income Pilots: Uses, Limitations and Design Principles." *Basic Income Studies* 16, no. 1 (2021): 75–99.

Standing, Guy, 2013. "Unconditional Basic Income: Two Pilots in Madhya Pradesh." Paper presented at the Conference on Unconditional Cash Transfers, New Delhi, India, May 30–31, 2013.

Tcherneva, Pavlina R. *The Case for a Job Guarantee*. Cambridge: John Wiley & Sons, 2020.

Torry, Malcolm, ed. *The Palgrave International Handbook of Basic Income*. Cham: Palgrave Macmillan, 2019.

van der Veen, Robert J., and Van Parijs, Philippe. "A Capitalist Road to Communism." *Theory and Society* 15, no. 5 (1986): 635–655.

Widerquist, Karl. "The Cost of Basic Income: Back-of-the-Envelope Calculations." *Basic Income Studies* 12, no. 2 (2017): 1–13.

Widerquist, Karl. *A Critical Analysis of Basic Income Experiments for Researchers, Policymakers, and Citizens*. Cham: Palgrave Macmillan, 2018.

Widerquist, Karl. "Exporting the Alaska Model to Alaska: How Big Could the Permanent Fund Be If the State Really Tried? And Can a Larger Fund Insulate an Oil-Exporter from the End of the Boom?" In *Exporting the Alaska Model: Adapting the Permanent Fund Dividend for Reform Around the World*, edited by Karl Widerquist and Michael W. Howard, 169–180. New York: Palgrave Macmillan, 2012.

Widerquist, Karl. "A Failure to Communicate: What (if Anything) Can We Learn from the Negative Income Tax Experiments?" *Journal of Socio-Economics* 34, no. 1 (2005): 49–81.

Widerquist, Karl. *Independence, Propertylessness, and Basic Income: A Theory of Freedom as the Power to Say No*. Cham: Palgrave Macmillan, 2013.

Widerquist, Karl. *The Problem of Property: Taking the Freedom of Nonowners Seriously*. Cham: Palgrave Macmillan, 2023.

Widerquist, Karl. "Three Waves of Basic Income Support." In *The Palgrave International Handbook of Basic Income*, edited by Malcolm Torry, 31–44. Cham: Palgrave Macmillan, 2019.

Widerquist, Karl. "Who Exploits Who?" *Political Studies* 54, no. 3 (2006): 444–464.

Widerquist, Karl, and Georg Arndt. "The Cost of Basic Income in the United Kingdom: A Microsimulation Analysis." *International Journal of Microsimulation* (forthcoming).

Widerquist, Karl, and Michael W. Howard, eds. *Alaska's Permanent Fund Dividend: Examining Its Suitability as a Model*. Cham: Palgrave Macmillan, 2012.

Widerquist, Karl, and Michael W. Howard. "Lessons from the Alaska Model." In *Alaska's Permanent Fund Dividend: Examining Its Suitability as Model*, edited by

Karl Widerquist and Michael W. Howard, 221–227. New York: Palgrave Macmillan, 2012.

Widerquist, Karl, and Grant S. McCall. *Prehistoric Myths in Modern Political Philosophy*. Edinburgh: Edinburgh University Press, 2017.

Widerquist, Karl, and Grant S. McCall. *The Prehistory of Private Property: Implications for Modern Political Theory*. Edinburgh: Edinburgh University Press, 2021.

Widerquist, Karl, José A. Noguera, Yannick Vanderborght, and Jurgen De Wispelaere, eds. *Basic Income: An Anthology of Contemporary Research*. Malden, MA: Wiley Blackwell, 2013.

Wilkinson, Richard G., and Kate Pickett. *The Spirit Level: Why More Equal Societies Almost Always Do Better*. London: Allen Lane, 2009.

FURTHER READING

Introduction to and General Overviews of UBI
Basic Income Studies, journal. As of 2021, sixteen volumes have been published since 2006.

De Wispelaere, Jurgen, and Lindsay Stirton, 2004. "The Many Faces of Universal Basic Income." *Political Quarterly* 75, no. 3 (2004): 266–274.

Downes, Amy, and Stewart Lansley. *It's Basic Income: The Global Debate*. Bristol: Policy Press, 2018.

Haagh, Louise. *The Case for Basic Income*. Cambridge: Polity, 2019.

Haagh, Louise. "Developmental Freedom and Social Order—Rethinking the Relation between Work and Equality." *Journal of Philosophical Economics* 1, no. 1 (2008): 119–160.

Lowrey, Annie. *Give People Money: How a Universal Basic Income Would End Poverty, Revolutionize Work, and Remake the World*. New York: Broadway Books, 2019.

Miller, Annie. *A Basic Income Pocketbook*. Edinburgh: Luath Press Limited, 2020.

Miller, Annie. *Essentials of Basic Income*, Edinburgh: Luath Press Limited, 2020.

Standing, Guy. *Basic Income: A Guide for the Open-Minded*. New Haven, CT: Yale University Press, 2017.

Torry, Malcolm. *101 Reasons for a Citizen's Income*. Bristol: Policy Press, 2015.

Torry, Malcolm. *The Feasibility of Citizen's Income*. Cham: Palgrave Macmillan, 2016.

Torry, Malcolm. *A Modern Guide to Citizen's Basic Income: A Multidisciplinary Approach*. Cheltenham: Edward Elgar, 2020.

Torry, Malcolm, ed. *The Palgrave International Handbook of Basic Income*. Cham: Palgrave Macmillan, 2019.

Torry, Malcolm. *Why We Need a Citizen's Basic Income: The Desirability, Feasibility and Implementation of an Unconditional Income*. Bristol: Policy Press, 2018.

van der Veen, Robert, and Loek Groot, eds. *Basic Income on the Agenda. Policies and Politics*. Amsterdam: Amsterdam University Press, 2000.

Van Parijs, Philippe, and Yannick Vanderborght. *Basic Income: A Radical Proposal for a Free Society and a Sane Economy*. Cambridge, MA: Harvard University Press, 2017.

Van Parijs, Philippe. *What's Wrong with a Free Lunch?* Edited by Joshua Cohen and Joel Rogers. Boston: Beacon Press, 2001.

Widerquist, Karl, and Michael A. Lewis. "The Basic Income Guarantee and the Goals of Equality, Efficiency, and Environmentalism." *International Journal of Environment, Workplace and Employment* 2, no. 1 (2006): 21–43.

Widerquist, Karl, Michael A. Lewis, and Steven Pressman, eds. *The Ethics and Economics of the Basic Income Guarantee*. Aldershot: Ashgate, 2005.

Widerquist, Karl, José A. Noguera, Yannick Vanderborght, and Jurgen De Wispelaere, eds. *Basic Income: An Anthology of Contemporary Research*. Malden, MA: Wiley Blackwell, 2013.

Automation, Postproductivism, and UBI

Santens, Scott. "The Real Story of Automation Beginning with One Simple Chart." Medium, October 24, 2017. https://medium.com/basic-income/the-real-story-of-automation-beginning-with-one-simple-chart-8b95f9bad71b.

Santens, Scott. "Self-Driving Trucks Are Going to Hit Us Like a Human-Driven Truck." Medium, May 14, 2015. https://medium.com/basic-income/self-driving-trucks-are-going-to-hit-us-like-a-human-driven-truck-b8507d9c5961.

Stern, Andrew. *Raising the Floor: How Universal Basic Income Can Renew Our Economy and Rebuild the American Dream*. New York: Public Affairs, 2016.

Widerquist, Karl, José A. Noguera, Yannick Vanderborght, and Jurgen De Wispelaere, eds. *Basic Income: An Anthology of Contemporary Research*. Malden, MA: Wiley Blackwell, 2013. See especially chapters 39–45.

Yang, Andrew. *The War on Normal People: The Truth About America's Disappearing Jobs and Why Universal Basic Income Is Our Future*. New York: Hachette Books, 2018.

The Alaska Dividend and UBI

Widerquist, Karl, and Michael W. Howard, eds. *Alaska's Permanent Fund Dividend: Examining Its Suitability as a Model*. Cham: Palgrave Macmillan, 2012.

Widerquist, Karl, and Michael W. Howard, eds. *Exporting the Alaska Model: Adapting the Permanent Fund Dividend for Reform Around the World*. Cham: Palgrave Macmillan, 2012.

Conditional Cash Transfers and UBI

Fiszbein, Ariel, and Norbert Schady, eds. *Conditional Cash Transfers: Reducing Present and Future Poverty*. Washington, DC: World Bank, 2009.

Hanlon, Joseph, Armando Barrientos, and David Hulme. *Just Give Money to the Poor: The Development Revolution from the Global South*. Boulder: Kumarian Press, 2010.

Cost and Economic Issues of UBI

Arndt, Georg, and Karl Widerquist. "Deceptively Simple: The Uselessness of Gross Cost in the Cost-Benefit Analysis of Universal Basic Income." *Maine Policy Review*, November 2019.

Atkinson, A. B. *Public Economics in Action: The Basic Income/Flat Tax Proposal*. Oxford: Clarendon Press, 1995.

Crocker, Geoff. *Basic Income and Sovereign Money: The Alternative to Economic Crisis and Austerity Policy*. Cham: Palgrave Macmillan, 2020.

Graeber, David. *Debt: The First 5,000 Years*. New York: Penguin, 2012.

Lansley, Stewart. *A Sharing Economy: How Social Wealth Funds Can Reduce Inequality and Help Balance the Books*. Bristol: Policy Press, 2016.

Martinelli, L. "A Basic Income Trilemma: Affordability, Adequacy, and the Advantages of Radically Simplified Welfare." *Journal of Social Policy* 49, no. 3 (2020): 461–482.

Santens, Scott. *Let There Be Money: Understanding Modern Monetary Theory and Basic Income*. Independently published, 2021.

Thomas, Alan. "Full Employment, Unconditional Basic Income and the Keynesian Critique of Rentier Capitalism." *Basic Income Studies* 15, no. 1 (2020): 1–38.

Van Parijs, Philippe, and Yannick Vanderborght. *Basic Income: A Radical Proposal for a Free Society and a Sane Economy*. Cambridge, MA: Harvard University Press, 2017. See especially chapter 6.

Widerquist, Karl. "The Cost of Basic Income: Back-of-the-Envelope Calculations," *Basic Income Studies*, no. 2 (2017): 1–13.

Widerquist, Karl, and Georg Arndt. "The Cost of Basic Income in the United Kingdom: A Microsimulation Analysis." *International Journal of Microsimulation* (forthcoming).

Widerquist, Karl, José A. Noguera, Yannick Vanderborght, and Jurgen De Wispelaere, eds. *Basic Income: An Anthology of Contemporary Research*. Malden, MA: Wiley Blackwell, 2013. See especially chapters 28–38.

The Effects of UBI

Haagh, L., and B. Rohregger. "Universal Basic Income Policies and Their Potential for Addressing Health Inequities." World Health Organization, June 2019. https://apps.who.int/iris/bitstream/handle/10665/346040/WHO-EURO-2019-3533-43292-60676-eng.pdf?sequence=3&isAllowed=y.

Hanlon, Joseph, Armando Barrientos, and David Hulme. *Just Give Money to the Poor: The Development Revolution from the Global South*. Boulder: Kumarian Press, 2010.

Fromm, Erich. "The Psychological Aspects of the Guaranteed Income." In *The Guaranteed Income: Next Step in Socioeconomic Evolution?*, edited by Robert Theobald, 183–193. New York: Doubleday, 1966.

Torry, Malcolm, ed. *The Palgrave International Handbook of Basic Income*. Cham: Palgrave Macmillan, 2019. See especially chapters 4–8.

Widerquist, Karl, José A. Noguera, Yannick Vanderborght, and Jurgen De Wispelaere, eds. *Basic Income: An Anthology of Contemporary Research*. Malden, MA: Wiley Blackwell, 2013.

The Ethics and Political Philosophy of UBI

Birnbaum, Simon. *Basic Income Reconsidered: Social Justice, Liberalism, and the Demands of Equality*. New York: Palgrave Macmillan, 2012.

Birnbaum, Simon, and Jurgen De Wispelaere. "Exit Strategy or Exit Trap? Basic Income and the 'Power to Say No' in the Age of Precarious Employment." *Socio-Economic Review* 19, no. 3 (July 2021): 909–927.

De Wispelaere, Jurgen, and Arto Laitinen. "Basic Income in the Recognition Order: Respect, Care, and Esteem." In *Redistribution, Recognition, and Beyond*, edited by Denise Celentano and Luigi Caranti, 9–26. London: Routledge, 2020.

De Wispelaere, Jurgen, and Leticia Morales. "Is There (or Should There Be) a Right to Basic Income?" *Philosophy and Social Criticism* 42, no. 9 (2016): 920–936.

Paine, Thomas. *Agrarian Justice*. Benjamin Franklin Bache, 1797.

Pettit, Philip. "A Republican Right to Basic Income?" *Basic Income Studies* 2, no. 2 (2008): 1–8.

Spence, Thomas. *The Rights of Infants*. Self-published, 1797.

Standing, Guy. *Plunder of the Commons: A Manifesto for Sharing Public Wealth*. London, Pelican, 2019.

Tideman, Nicolaus, and Peter Vallentyne. "Left-Libertarianism and a Global Rent Payment." In *Basic Income: An Anthology of Contemporary Research*, edited by Karl Widerquist, José A. Noguera, Yannick Vanderborght, and Jurgen De Wispelaere, 43–48. Oxford: Wiley-Blackwell, 2013.

Torry, Malcolm, ed. *The Palgrave International Handbook of Basic Income*. Cham: Palgrave Macmillan, 2019. See especially chapters 22–26

van der Veen, Robert J., and Van Parijs, Philippe. "A Capitalist Road to Communism." *Theory and Society* 15 (1986): 635–655.

Van Donselaar, Gijs. *The Right to Exploit: Parasitism, Scarcity, and Basic Income*. Oxford: Oxford University Press, 2009.

Van Parijs, Philippe, ed. *Arguing for Basic Income: Ethical Foundations for a Radical Reform*. New York: Verso, 1992.

Van Parijs, Philippe. *Real Freedom for All: What (if Anything) Can Justify Capitalism?* Oxford: Oxford University Press, 1995.

Van Parijs, Philippe. "Why Surfers Should be Fed: The Liberal Case for an Unconditional Basic Income." *Philosophy & Public Affairs* 20 (1991): 101–131.

Van Parijs, Philippe, and Yannick Vanderborght. *Basic Income: A Radical Proposal for a Free Society and a Sane Economy*. Cambridge, MA: Harvard University Press, 2017. See especially chapter 5.

Waldron, Jeremy. "Homelessness and the Issue of Freedom." In *Liberal Rights*, edited by Jeremy Waldron, 309–338. Cambridge: Cambridge University Press, 1993.

Widerquist, Karl. *Independence, Propertylessness, and Basic Income: A Theory of Freedom as the Power to Say No*. Cham: Palgrave Macmillan, 2013.

Widerquist, Karl. "My Own Private Basic Income." In *It's Basic Income: The Global Debate*, edited by Amy Downes and Stewart Lansley, 48–53. Bristol: Policy Press, 2018.

Widerquist, Karl. "The People's Endowment." In *Institutions for Future Generations*, edited by Axel Gosseries and Inigo Gonzalez, 312–333. Oxford: Oxford University Press, 2016.

Widerquist, Karl. "The Physical Basis of Voluntary Trade," *Human Rights Review* 11, no. 1 (2010): 83–103.

Widerquist, Karl. *The Problem of Property: Taking the Freedom of Nonowners Seriously*. Cham: Palgrave Macmillan, 2023.

Widerquist, Karl. "Who Exploits Who?" *Political Studies* 54, no. 3 (2006): 444–464.

Widerquist, Karl, Michael Anthony Lewis, and Steven Pressman, eds. *The Ethics and Economics of the Basic Income Guarantee*. Aldershot: Ashgate, 2005.

Widerquist, Karl, and Grant S. McCall. *Prehistoric Myths in Modern Political Philosophy*. Edinburgh: Edinburgh University Press, 2017.

Widerquist, Karl, and Grant S. McCall. *The Prehistory of Private Property: Implications for Modern Political Theory*. Edinburgh: Edinburgh University Press, 2021.

Widerquist, Karl, José A. Noguera, Yannick Vanderborght, and Jurgen De Wispelaere, eds. *Basic Income: An Anthology of Contemporary Research*. Malden, MA: Wiley Blackwell, 2013.

Wright, Erik O., ed. *Redesigning Distribution: Basic Income and Stakeholder Grants as Cornerstones of a More Egalitarian Capitalism*. New York: Verso, 2006.

Experiments on UBI
Standing, Guy. "Basic Income Pilots: Uses, Limitations and Design Principles." *Basic Income Studies* 16, no. 1 (2021): 75–99.

Torry, Malcolm, ed. *The Palgrave International Handbook of Basic Income*. Cham: Palgrave Macmillan, 2019. See especially chapters 15–21.

Widerquist, Karl. "The Bottom Line in a Basic Income Experiment." *Basic Income Studies* 1, no. 2 (2006): 1–5.

Widerquist, Karl. *A Critical Analysis of Basic Income Experiments for Researchers, Policymakers, and Citizens*. Cham: Palgrave Macmillan, 2018.

Widerquist, Karl. "Further Reflections on Basic Income Experiments," *Ethical Perspectives* 28, no. 1 (March 2021): 103–115.

Widerquist, Karl. "The Negative Income Tax Experiments of the 1970s." In *The Palgrave International Handbook of Basic Income*, edited by Malcolm Torry, 313–318. Cham: Palgrave Macmillan, 2019.

Widerquist, Karl. "Possibilities and Pitfalls of Basic Income Experiments." *Ethical Perspectives* 28, no. 1 (March 2021): 7–16.

Feminism, the Family, and UBI
Funiciello, T. *The Tyranny of Kindness*. New York: Grove/Atlantic, 1994.

Gheaus, Anca. "The Feminist Argument against Supporting Care." *Journal of Practical Ethics* 8, no. 1 (June 2020): 87–113.

Sloman, Peter, Daniel Zamora Vargas, and Pedro Ramos Pinto, eds. *The Intellectual History of Basic Income*. Cham: Palgrave Macmillan, 2021.

Robeyns, Ingrid. "Will a Basic Income Do Justice to Women?" *Analyse & Kritik* 23, no. 1 (2001): 88–105.

Widerquist, Karl, José A. Noguera, Yannick Vanderborght, and Jurgen De Wispelaere, eds. *Basic Income: An Anthology of Contemporary Research*. Malden, MA: Wiley Blackwell, 2013. See especially chapters 21–27.

Woolf, Virginia. *A Room of One's Own*. Toronto: Joe Books, 2016.

The History of UBI
Theobald, Robert, ed. *The Guaranteed Income*. New York: Doubleday, 1966.

Torry, Malcolm. *Basic Income: A History*. Cheltenham: Edward Elgar, 2021.

Sloman, Peter, Daniel Zamora Vargas, and Pedro Ramos Pinto, eds. *The Intellectual History of Basic Income*. Cham: Palgrave Macmillan, 2021.

Van Parijs, Philippe, and Yannick Vanderborght. *Basic Income: A Radical Proposal for a Free Society and a Sane Economy*. Cambridge, MA: Harvard University Press, 2017. See especially chapter 4.

Widerquist, Karl. "Three Waves of Basic Income Support." In *The Palgrave International Handbook of Basic Income*, ed. Malcolm Torry, 31–44. Cham: Palgrave Macmillan, 2019.

Implementation and Institutions

De Wispelaere, Jurgen, and Lindsay Stirton. "The Administrative Efficiency of Basic Income." *Policy and Politics* 39, no. 1 (2011): 115–132.

De Wispelaere, Jurgen, and Lindsay Stirton. "A Disarmingly Simple Idea? Practical Bottlenecks in Implementing a Universal Basic Income." *International Social Security Review* 65, no. 2 (2012): 103–121.

De Wispelaere, Jurgen, and Lindsay Stirton. "When Basic Income Meets Professor Pangloss: Ignoring Public Administration and Its Perils." *Political Quarterly* 88, no. 2 (2017): 298–305.

Torry, Malcolm, ed. *The Palgrave International Handbook of Basic Income*. Cham: Palgrave Macmillan, 2019. See especially chapters 9–12.

Widerquist, Karl, José A. Noguera, Yannick Vanderborght, and Jurgen De Wispelaere, eds. *Basic Income: An Anthology of Contemporary Research*. Malden, MA: Wiley Blackwell, 2013. See especially chapters 46–64.

The Politics and Political Economy of UBI

Caputo, Richard, ed. *Basic Income Guarantee and Politics*. New York: Palgrave, 2012.

Davala, Sarath, Renana Jhabvala, Soumy Mehta, and Guy Standing. *Basic Income: A Transformative Policy for India*. London: Bloomsbury, 2015.

De Wispelaere, Jurgen. "The Struggle for Strategy: On the Politics of the Basic Income Proposal." *Politics* 36, no. 2 (2016): 131–141.

De Wispelaere, Jurgen, and Leticia Morales. "The Stability of Basic Income: A Constitutional Solution for a Political Problem?" *Journal of Public Policy* 36, no. 4 (2016): 521–545.

Funiciello, T. *The Tyranny of Kindness*. New York: Grove/Atlantic, 1994.

Haagh, L. "Democracy, Public Finance, and Property Rights in Economic Stability: How More Horizontal Capitalism Upscales Freedom for All." *Polity* 44, no. 4 (2012): 1–46.

Standing, Guy. *Global Labour Flexibility: Seeking Distributive Justice*. London: Macmillan, 1999.

Standing, Guy. *The Precariat: The New Dangerous Class*. London: Bloomsbury, 2011.

Torry, Malcolm, ed. *The Palgrave International Handbook of Basic Income*. Cham: Palgrave Macmillan, 2019. See especially chapters 13–14.

Van Parijs, Philippe, and Yannick Vanderborght. 2017. *Basic Income: A Radical Proposal for a Free Society and a Sane Economy*. Cambridge, MA: Harvard University Press, 2017. See especially chapter 7.

Widerquist, Karl, José A. Noguera, Yannick Vanderborght, and Jurgen De Wispelaere, eds. *Basic Income: An Anthology of Contemporary Research*. Malden, MA: Wiley Blackwell, 2013. See especially chapters 65–74.

Right-Libertarianism and UBI

Fleischer, Miranda Perry, and Otto Lehto. "Libertarian Perspectives on Basic Income." In *The Palgrave International Handbook of Basic Income*, edited by Malcolm Torry, 439–458. Cham: Palgrave Macmillan, 2019.

Friedman, Milton. "The Case for the Negative Income Tax: A View from the Right." In *Issues of American Public Policy*, edited by J. H. Bunzel, 111–120. Englewood Cliffs, NJ: Prentice-Hall, 1968.

Friedman, Milton, and Rose Friedman. *Free to Choose: A Personal Statement*. New York: Harcourt Brace Jovanovich, 1980.

Nell, Guinevere Liberty, ed. *Basic Income and the Free Market*. New York: Palgrave Macmillan, 2013.

Websites

Basic Income Earth Network, BasicIncome.org. A great resource for international research and news.

Basic Income Today: The Universal Basic Income News Hub, BasicIncomeToday.com. A US-based UBI news website.

Center for Guaranteed Income Research at the University of Pennsylvania, PennCGIR.org. An applied research center specializing in cash-transfer research, evaluation, pilot design, and narrative change.

Income Movement, IncomeMovement.org. A US-based activist group working to pass UBI legislation.

Karl Widerquist's Research Channel (YouTube), www.youtube.com/channel/UCI8CNYDttQ2bk0KK-KEOc7w. Videos of interviews, lectures, and speeches by the author.

Research Website of Karl Widerquist, Widerquist.com. This website includes links to free versions of most of my research and writing.

Scott Santens, ScottSantens.com. Santens is a writer and full-time UBI advocate. He is one of the world's the most prolific journalists focusing on UBI. His website covers a wide range of UBI-related topics and makes them easy to understand.

Scott Santens (YouTube channel), https://www.youtube.com/c/ScottSantens. Includes his list of the "Best Universal Basic Income Videos."

UBI Center, UBIcenter.org. A group of scholars who publish open-source research on UBI.

US Basic Income Guarantee Network, USBIG.net. A great resource for US research and news.

Page numbers followed by t indicate tables.

KARL WIDERQUIST is a professor of philosophy specializing in *distributive justice*: the ethics of who has what. He holds doctorates in political theory and economics. He has published dozens of scholarly articles, and several books, including *The Prehistory of Private Property* (with Grant S. McCall); *A Critical Analysis of Basic Income Experiments*; *Prehistoric Myths in Modern Political Philosophy* (with Grant S. McCall); and *Independence, Propertylessness, and Basic Income: A Theory of Freedom as the Power to Say No*. The *Atlantic Monthly* described Widerquist as a leader of the worldwide basic income movement.